STRAIGHT
FROM THE
HEART

★

My Life in Politics
and Other Places

★

ANN RICHARDS

with Peter Knobler

SIMON AND SCHUSTER

New York London Toronto Sydney Tokyo

Simon and Schuster
Simon & Schuster Building
Rockefeller Center
1230 Avenue of the Americas
New York, New York 10020

Designed by Laurie Jewell
Manufactured in the Untied States of America

10   9   8   7   6   5   4   3   2   1

Library of Congress Cataloging-in-Publication Data

Richards, Ann, date.
Straight from the heart.

1. Richards, Ann, date.   2. Politicians—
United States—Biography.   3. Democratic Party (U.S.)
—Biography.   4. Texas—Politics and government—
1951-   .   5. Presidents—United States—Election—
1988.   I. Knobler, Peter.   II. Title.
E840.8.R49A3   1989   973.927′092   [B]   89-21633
ISBN 0-671-68073-0

ACKNOWLEDGMENTS

★

MY THANKS TO Jody Gent, David Richards, Jane Hickie, Jack Martin, Chula Reynolds, Mark McKinnon, and Pat Cole, who read the manuscript, gave good advice, and filled in the blanks. Alice Mayhew and Esther Newburg were patient and encouraging. Gail Olson transcribed quickly. Peter Knobler adapted wonderfully from New York jargon and sports to Texas drawl and politics.

And my friend Bud Shrake lent a sympathetic and patient ear through it all.

Cecile, Dan, Clark, and Ellen,
my children, who, like the tail on a kite,
have given me balance in the
buffeting winds—A.R.

★

For Jane and Daniel—P.K.

PREFACE

★

MY DADDY USED TO SAY, "She looks like she was rode hard and put up wet," and that is about the way I feel on finishing this book. Telling the story of your life is not an easy task. Reliving the tough times is painful, but the recollection of good times with my friends and family warmed me like a blanket.

The thread of my political life is the consistent issue of civil rights. While political party struggles, campaigns, and personalities came and went, the commitment to equality is a constant. I thank God that I live in a country where that fight is possible and the cause progresses.

There are a lot more stories where these came from, but I hope that those recounted here will give a flavor of what it is like to be a woman, a mother, and grandmother who cares passionately about our government and who loves the state of Texas.

1

★

IF my Mama in Waco can't understand what I'm talking about, no one else can. I make a lot of speeches and I keep that in mind all the time.

It's not that my Mama's dumb, or that she's the lowest common denominator. She's smart, she's got a lot of common sense. She doesn't have to have it explained to her twice. But don't try to speak to her in jargon. Tell it to her straight.

Most people have learned a second language; usually it's specific to their occupation. That's true of bankers and lawyers and doctors and truckers and everybody else. It is particularly true of people in government; they speak in alphabet soup, gobbledygook. My Mama doesn't fit in any of those categories, and when I speak I want it to be something that she can understand straight out. Language should bind us, not divide us.

That's why, when I got off the stage at the Omni in Atlanta after delivering the Keynote Address at the Democratic National Convention, I really wanted to know what my Mama thought about it.

Speaking in public is a very personal piece of business. Giving a good speech, especially one with some passion and emotion, you're revealing a lot about yourself. You're putting yourself in a very vulnerable position. It's sort of like Lady Godiva riding down Main Street without clothes on. Or stepping up on a scale and getting weighed. There's every possibility in the world that you'll be found wanting.

My parents live in Waco and had gone to a watch party that the Democratic Party had held at a downtown hotel to see the speech. A local Waco television station had made arrangements for us to have a split-screen hookup between Atlanta and Waco. It was good television for them and a chance for me to get through to my folks.

The pathways in and underneath the Omni in Atlanta were a maze of wires and cables, as if they were carrying some kind of national pulse that everybody kept tripping over. You just can't imagine what the working conditions are like for the local television press at these conventions. They are sharing equipment; the space each station is allotted is no bigger than a closet; and each interviewer and camera crew is divided off from the next one by either a thin drapery or nothing at all. On TV it looks like each newsperson has some fabulous access and personal angle; in fact, the correspondents are just about butting thighs.

And so I got to talk with my folks. There were no monitors, which means that I couldn't see them and they couldn't see me, but we could hear each other and it was a nice thing to do.

There's no great secret to good political television. Most reporters want to know the same information, and the people they are interviewing generally have one set of facts and viewpoints they want to get over. The trick to doing well on television is keeping it fresh, remembering that there are real people watching, and that they have real feelings. The temptation is to talk to the camera; I try real hard to talk to the people instead.

The news announcer introduced us to the audience and said, "Well, Mr. Willis, when you told your daughter that she could do anything she wanted to do if she just worked hard enough, did you ever dream that she would be doing something like this?" My Daddy chortled, "Why, hell, I didn't even know there *was* a this!"

My Mama and Daddy said that they were proud of me and they were glad that I got to do the speech, all of that. It was pretty much what you would expect of a public family moment.

I called them the next day to tell them what a good job they had done in their television appearance and that I was real pleased that the Waco station had done that hookup. I knew that they had probably been nervous, having had to talk on camera.

I shouldn't have worried. My Mama said, "Well, Ann, it was just wonderful." She sounded nicely excited, like I had hoped she would. "I just never had such a good time. We really enjoyed it!" It seemed like the excitement was still with her.

"But what you don't know," she went on, "you'll never guess what happened. Something that was really wonderful last night."

Texans are proud of their own, and I had been getting calls and congratulations all morning. I knew my Mama was going to tell me something someone had said that was complimentary about the speech. I warmed to the phone.

"No, Mama, what?"

She said, "Coming out of that interview at the television station . . . we met the weatherman! I've been listening to him for ten years and I never dreamed I'd meet him in person!"

The Keynote Address is the first major statement of purpose and direction at the Democratic National Convention. It's a speaker's dream. Everybody who cares even the slightest bit about politics can be counted on to watch, or at least will hear about what you have to say. I had never even considered giving it.

When it comes to speaking engagements, I've got a pretty full plate. They're not necessarily political speeches, they can fall into any number of categories: education, criminal justice, the economy, the state's financial picture, where women are going, alcoholism, drug abuse, you name it. I am asked to give a lot of speeches and I try to talk to as many people as I can.

But three weeks before the Democratic Convention I had planned to take a week off. The board of directors of the Foundation for Women's Resources gathers each year for its annual planning session. We eat healthy food, get plenty of exercise, and meet and talk about what we would like the foundation to do in the coming year. We all look forward to it.

I was on my way to Houston one Friday morning and I called the office from the airport to pick up my messages and return some calls before I got on the plane. Nancy Kohler, my assistant, told me that Paul Kirk had called and wanted to talk to me. There were several minutes before my plane was due to leave. I called him.

Paul Kirk, at the time, was the national chairman of the Democratic Party. He said, "I'm calling to find out where you're going to be next Monday."

"I'm planning to be out of town for a board meeting," I told him.

"Well, Ann," he said, "I have to check it out with a couple of places, but I think you'll be invited to deliver the Keynote Address at the Democratic National Convention."

I was standing there on the linoleum at a pay phone in the airport and I was floored.

"You're kidding me."

"No," he said, "we think you're the logical choice."

I felt certain that I would be asked to do something at the convention, because I am female and they need to have females play a role and there are simply not that many of us in politics. But this was a great deal more than I had expected.

"Well," I told him, "that is simply incredible. Never, ever, in my wildest dreams, would I have thought that I would be invited to do such a thing."

Paul said, "Don't say anything to anyone about it, but I think this thing is pretty much a done deal."

"You can count on me. I won't breathe a word."

"If it does come about," he continued, "you can't be out of town when it hits the press." This was classic politics; the next step from honor is logistics.

I was so naive, not having ever had an experience like that before, that I had no idea what he meant by "when it hits the press." I was the treasurer of the state of Texas and I had been elected to office in four different races; I just figured there would be a lot of press calls that day that I would have to deal with.

"Oh, really? Can't I do it long-distance?"

"No, you won't be able to do that."

"Well, okay, I won't go."

By the time I phoned the office for messages that afternoon the story had leaked. The *Atlanta Constitution* had called wanting to do an interview about my doing the Keynote speech.

Now, the talk of my making the governor's race was pretty much an open case, and the political tides never stop churning. Over the weekend I was told that Jim Mattox, my likely primary opponent, had tried to dissuade Paul Kirk from extending the invitation to speak. The reply from the national office was, "Well, the governor's race is a long way off, and we have no intention of getting involved in it, but the decision is made."

And so, on Monday morning, the announcement came from Paul Kirk that I would be the Keynote speaker. And my life was completely overturned.

15

I had a little two-person political office and it was overwhelmed. The calls started coming in for interviews. Television crews, radio interviewers, national stringers, freelance writers all wanted to follow me around. I was staggered by all of it. I thought it would last maybe a day or two and then it would all die down, but it never quit. *Newsweek,* the *Boston Globe,* the *New York Times* . . . I was going to Stephenville, Texas, to place a historic marker, speak to the Optimist Club and attend a local reception, and here we were chartering a plane for an entourage of press!

I knew I was receiving a great honor, but there was not a moment to stop and reflect about where I was going or what I was going to do, because I was giving the next interview. And then when I'd get back to the office there would be a jillion telephone calls I had to return. One day we had reporters scheduled every thirty minutes from twelve noon till six o'clock at night. One after the other—radio, television, newspapers.

It was mayhem. I was treasurer of Texas, a public official, but I had never thought to have an unlisted phone number and most people respected my privacy. Not anymore. All kinds of people started calling. My phone rang about nine o'clock at night and it was a woman who said that she'd been cleaning out a trunk and ran across an "All the Way with LBJ" button and couldn't recall who his vice president was, and she just knew I'd remember. I got an unlisted phone number.

By the end of the first week it became apparent to me that this was never-ending. I started getting nervous. There is something very gratifying about being chosen for such an important and prestigious assignment, but I actually had to give this speech. The euphoria rapidly evaporated and the task at hand loomed up like a specter.

Meanwhile, we were getting drafts of speeches from total strangers. People were calling wanting to volunteer to write the speech. People were calling wanting to get paid to help write the speech. People were calling to advise how to avoid having someone else take credit for having written the speech that did not yet exist. You know. Bedlam.

I spoke with Jane Hickie, my campaign adviser, and said, "We've got to have a pro here, we really do. I have a general notion of how I want the speech to go and what we need to say. I think I know how to open and close it, which are the two tough parts. But we need a wordsmith."

I did some calling around. Bob Strauss, the former chairman of the national party, recommended a speechwriter named John Sherman. John had written for Senator Robert Byrd and had assignments for several people at the convention already, and he flew down to Austin and met with us.

Suzanne Coleman has always written a lot of speeches for me, so she sat in. She also works at the Treasury, so we were very careful that any political writing she did was on her own time and at home. Suzanne brought some of my old speeches and her first draft, and John took it all in and went back to Virginia to begin.

I was still trying to keep up with the schedule I had already committed to before all this frenzy began, plus my regular work. So I decided to Let go, Let God, and Let John, and he put together a draft of the speech and sent it back to me. There were pieces in it I liked, pieces in it I didn't care for, so I did an edit on that and faxed it back to him. The political office fax machine never stopped.

Mary Beth Rogers, a good political writer who was also deputy treasurer, got into it on her own time. Jane got into it. Cathy Bonner is a public relations consultant, and we went out to her place and began working on John's draft and the other bits and pieces we had. It was rapidly turning into real patchwork.

17

One day I came into the office and Mary Beth said, "We have just received a letter that is your speech." It was from a woman in Lorena, Texas. I said, "We'll have to get in touch with her. If we use this letter the press will make that woman's life miserable. We need to tell her in advance what will happen if she is willing to let us use it." I had seen this press rush and I know that to someone who isn't in the public eye, it could be very painful.

We called and the woman said she was delighted and flattered. We agreed to keep her name confidential, but told her that the heat was going to be considerable and that the press was going to come looking for her. She said, well, that was all right, go ahead and use it.

I was also calling those people I knew who could write lines. I wasn't looking for a speech from them, just for any good lines they'd got. We called Jane Wagner, who writes with Lily Tomlin. I called Erma Bombeck and Liz Carpenter. For years, George Christian had written speeches for Lyndon Johnson. I called George. I called Harry McPherson in Washington, D.C.; Harry also wrote a lot of speeches for Johnson. He said that I had to be aware of who my audience was, and who I would be speaking with on the television. I called Barbara Jordan.

We called Harrison Hickman, a political adviser, to ask if he would write a profile of a married couple living in the suburbs who were in their late thirties or early forties and were trying to raise children. That's who I wanted to speak to. Harrison wrote that profile.

I called Ted Sorensen. I didn't even know Ted Sorensen, but I knew he was a whale of a speechwriter. I know he thought, "Who is this woman?" But I really wanted advice from the best people I could get.

We got videotapes of Mario Cuomo's 1984 Keynote Address and Barbara Jordan's 1976 Keynote, and I took those home and played them on the VCR and quickly became very depressed. What they had had to say was so substantive, so powerful. What did I have to say?

The morning after it was announced that I would be giving the Keynote Address, Mario Cuomo had called. It was one of the nicest things anyone has ever done for me. Mario's Keynote Address to the 1984 Democratic Convention had been electrifying, a smooth and brilliant combination of personality, language, and vision. He told me how he'd felt when he had been called and invited to give the speech: Terrified, as he knew I was. He'd thought, "What have I got to say?"

Mario has a remarkably soothing way about him. He told me he had finally broken through when he had asked the people who worked around him what he ought to say. Then he had written a draft and read it to his co-workers.

One of the best pieces of advice he'd gotten, he told me, came from an elevator operator or janitor at the state capitol building in Albany, who had said, "Governor, you didn't mention your father in that speech. You usually talk about your father."

It was that kind of wonderful, serious conversation about, "I know how you feel, and don't worry, you'll be all right."

And, of course, there was the What Will She Wear? question. Friends from all over Texas started sending clothes: Betty McKool and Janelle Ellis went shopping in Dallas and shipped in boxes of suits and dresses; Sarah Lake canvassed the stores in San Antonio and drove up to Austin with cartons full; Raye Carrington made an intensive browse of Austin to see what she could find; Grace Jones drove down a rack from Salado.

So we'd get clothes in and I'd barely have time to look at them, then we'd box them up and send them back. In an odd kind of way, this was a vital decision; if I didn't look right, there was every chance that half the people I was trying to reach wouldn't hear me.

Barbara Mikulski, now senator from Maryland, called and said, "Ann, there is a woman in Washington, D.C., who is absolutely fabulous with makeup. Her name is Lillian Brown, she's going to be at the convention, you need to call and talk to her. She made me up for debates and she took off ten pounds, ten years, and ten thousand wrinkles."

Lillian Brown was very nice, said she'd be glad to do it, and also volunteered to help find something to wear. She asked about size and style and color and price. I told her that blues are good colors. I said the main thing was that it should be an American-made dress. I didn't care whether it was a "designer dress" or not but I wanted it made in America. I have very strong feelings about that. I drive an American car, and where it is at all possible I buy American goods. American business depends on American consumption.

Lillian Brown called back the next day and said, "I have found a very simple three-piece dress in sort of an aqua. Adele Simpson. It's silk and I think it'll be a perfect camera color." I said, "Here's my charge account number. Send it."

Neal Spelce had coached Mario Cuomo on the use of the TelePrompTer in 1984. We got hold of Neal, who agreed to go with me to Atlanta and teach me how to be a great communicator.

Jane Hickie, meanwhile, was, in her usual fashion, doing an unbelievably adept job of organization. She called Gordon Wynne, who had been in charge of the logistics of the Democratic Convention since the beginning of time, and said, "Gordon, will you be our Convention Director in Atlanta?" Gordon said he would be delighted.

On top of having to speak, I had been elevated to the rank of Dignitary, and with that mighty position came the need for a traveling organization. We needed people to deal with the telephones, the Xeroxing, the word processors, the fax machines, the watch parties at home, receptions, cars, security, press, and other dignitaries. We needed someone to deal with the Texas delegation; there were hundreds of requests for floor passes, especially on the night of the speech. We needed a place for people to come by and say hello, and people to take care of the people who were going to come by and say hello. Nancy Kohler had worked with me for years and knew how to handle chaos, so she had to come along. My daughter Cecile, her husband, Kirk Adams, and my granddaughter Lily were coming from California. My children Dan, Clark, and Ellen were coming. We needed hotel rooms for all of these people. Gordon Wynne and the staff took care of all of that.

And I still had to come up with something to say.

The day before we were supposed to leave for Atlanta we were all sitting in Cathy's office cutting up this speech and piecing it together, and I was not at all happy. It didn't have the flow, the feeling that I knew it needed. There wasn't a conversational tone. But, for better or worse, we got something together and faxed it again to John.

John Sherman was due to fax us more or less his final draft when he called to say that his computer had eaten the speech. He couldn't get it out. The guy from the computer company was over there that moment and they were working on it, but he was afraid that the speech—and all of our work since the moment I had been chosen to deliver it—was gone forever.

It was funny. I mean, I just thought, "Whatever can happen will happen. And it's happening." You can rail and rant and do all you want to do, but all you do is get yourself in an uproar. I really do have an ultimate faith that if things are supposed to turn out well, they'll turn out well.

So we left for Atlanta with no speech.

I got off the plane in the Atlanta airport and there were more newspeople and television cameras. Just like I'd seen on TV with other people. But this was focused at me! It was really a peculiar feeling.

You feel like they've made a mistake. That really they don't understand that you're not that important. It was my first true moment in the eye of the media storm, and it took some getting used to. At first just the newness of it was a little distracting. But hour by hour, as it wasn't going away, I settled into it. I began to think of the attention as just part of my job: this is just what I do and this crush is going to be part of it. The best you can do is to be candid, answer the questions the best that you can, and be good-natured about it.

They didn't know that at that moment I really was unprepared.

At the Omni, the podium was still being built when I arrived, the boards were literally being put in place as I walked on them. And underneath, out of view, there was a rehearsal room that was identical to the podium above. The TelePrompTers were in place, the podium, the lights. The technicians could arrange it so that you could determine the height you needed, the angle of the TelePrompTer lenses. They were extremely nice to me. Perhaps they realized how terrified I was.

Of course, as well as being a political gathering, a convention is a series of parties. Just because I had taken on this Keynote didn't mean I should back out of the commitments I had already made. And I had a full schedule.

There was a breakfast in my honor. I can't even tell you who was there, I was just traveling in a daze. I couldn't go anywhere without a huge trail of cameras and microphones and the people attracted by the cameras and microphones.

And meanwhile, we were working on the speech. At one point we had a very full room: Neal Spelce, John Sherman,

Suzanne Coleman, Mary Beth, Jane. Harrison Hickman was in and out. Cecile's husband, Kirk, was there. Harrison and John Sherman agreed that they would go off and write something and bring it back, but finally, on Saturday afternoon, late, I said, "You know, I'm really not happy with this." I was supposed to deliver this stirring oratory on Monday night.

Now, mind you, before we had reached this point there had been a jillion drafts of this speech. Nancy Kohler was typing and lines were coming in from all over, and they were plugging in segments we'd pick up here and there.

They all looked at me and said, "Well, what do you want to say?" I mean, they were pretty disgusted with me, and I don't blame them. I just felt like we were being too eloquent, too lofty-sounding. I wanted to speak so that my Mama understood what I was talking about.

Right from the beginning of the speech I wanted to make it clear that "We're about to have some fun." I wanted an overall feeling that made people know that politics does not have to be all gloom and doom and lofty rhetoric, that it is really personal, and that it's fun. That it is, next to baseball and football, the All-American pastime.

So I sat there at the table and said, "We're going to tell how the cow ate the cabbage."

I knew several things that had to be done in the speech. I wanted to say, from the beginning, that I know that my accent is different from yours, and for the majority of you in that television audience I know I don't sound like you. And I wanted to say it in a way that would be funny so that they would accept me and my accent.

I wanted to say, also right away, I realize that I am female, and that not many females get to do what I am doing, but I hope you will listen to me. And I wanted to say something that would make the women feel good about me being there, and get that issue settled so that I did not focus on women's issues again and again in the speech.

I wanted to say, "I am no different than you are. All you people sitting out there in your living rooms listening to this person speak, I am an American who cares intensely about her country and its politics."

So—"After listening to George Bush all these years, I figured you needed to know what a real Texas accent sounds like." It's a funny line and it makes its point.

"Twelve years ago, Barbara Jordan, another Texas woman, made the Keynote Address to this convention . . . and two women in 160 years is about par for the course." That recognizes I'm female and I know this is a rare thing, and that we can recognize it, and laugh about it.

"But, if you give us the chance, we can perform. After all, Ginger Rogers did everything that Fred Astaire did. She just did it backwards and in high heels." I've used that line in speeches for years and years, and I have no idea of the real origin of it. I think I got it from Linda Ellerbee.

I met Linda Ellerbee down in the rehearsal room during one practice session and she said, "I heard you are going to use the Ginger Rogers line." I told her, "I am. Would you like me to attribute it to you?" She said, "No, don't worry about that. I don't even think it was original with me." I heard later that she got it from someone on an airplane.

I used the line about the guy who yelled out from the bleachers, "Make that basket, birdlegs"—which I have used in speeches many times before—because it says, "I am imperfect and I have some sense of myself."

Okay, it seemed to me, we've got all those lines behind us now and we've already done a great deal. We've said a lot in about five lines. And now we have them ready to listen.

I knew that I wanted to end my speech with something

about my granddaughter, Lily. It was a way to span generations, to talk about how we look into the future in a very personal way. Because that's really what it all boils down to; we can talk all we want about concepts and ideas and problems, but basically what we want is a future that is good for our grandchildren.

We usually have our children when we're young, when we don't have the patience to sit and live on their time; once we've read them a book we expect them to go to bed. The older we get, the more we enjoy those moments rather than trying to avoid them. In chatting with John Sherman the first night he had come down to Austin I had told him about Lily and me, sitting on the floor, rolling a ball back and forth, back and forth. John turned around and made that the visual image that ended the speech.

All that remained was the body of the speech, and we had a little over a day to write it.

I began to talk about the Democratic Party, the one that I had grown up knowing. I was talking to that family that doesn't really think politics makes any difference to them. They obviously don't because they don't participate. Not even half the population votes. This was the Democratic National Convention Keynote Address: it ought to say what this party stands for, it ought to say Why I Am a Democrat.

I had a checklist of things I wanted to include in the speech. I wanted to make sure we said something about education and that we included teachers. I didn't want to talk about education as an idea, but I wanted to talk about it from the point of view of the people who were involved in it. I wanted to talk about the environment, clean water, clean air. Very simple concepts that everyone understands, that the government controls.

I wanted to say that I felt the administration had misled us, that the billions of dollars we had poured into defense had gone into the pockets of some greedy people. And that we believe very strongly in defending this nation, but it doesn't make sense to us when we spend our hard-earned tax dollars on systems that don't work. That's when we came up with "tanks that won't shoot and planes that won't fly." I sat there and shook my head and said, "That old dog won't hunt."

And all the time I was talking, they were writing.

By this time Jane Wagner had gotten exercised. She had decided that this speech was important and she was going fax crazy, most of it wonderful stuff. It was great moral support from a real professional. The "silver foot" line came in from Jane. I don't know who said it originally—several people have taken credit for it—I don't have any idea. I got it from Jane.

By this time it was getting pretty late. I was tired. I had done a full day of shaking and howdying and visiting with people and rehearsing. So they all said to me, "Okay, now you go on to bed and we'll work it out."

I went to bed and they stayed up all night. And the next morning, there was the speech under my door when I got up.

There was some question about whether to keep the "silver foot" line. I think maybe Harrison Hickman said it was an old line, everybody knew it. I said, "Well, I don't know it. And if I don't know it, Mama in Waco doesn't know it either." Kirk came to me and said, "Don't let them talk you into taking that line out. It's too good." So I said okay.

There was never any intention in that speech to slam George Bush or Ronald Reagan. I think negative speeches are very hard to carry off, and they leave you with a bad taste. I felt that line was good because it's a lampoon line, like a newspaper editorial cartoonist's line. And it's also very funny.

I spent hours of time rehearsing versions of the speech. It had to sound casual, conversational, but that took work.

You had to book the rehearsal room in advance and you

didn't dare miss your appointment. There was always a line waiting to get inside, and a little holding area outside the room with all kinds of people coming in and out. Ted Kennedy came through, Bill Clinton from Arkansas, Barbara Mikulski, Jim Wright. It was all very exciting and fun, a combination of casual good humor and formal terror, like a first prom.

The TelePrompTer staff were tireless. I'd come in one day with one speech and they would put it into the computer and print hard copies for me, and the next thing you know I'd come in with a whole new one. They were so patient and so kind.

We had the rehearsal room booked every day from the time I got there, beginning on Friday and running all the way through Monday. In an hour I could usually get through it once and a half, and I must have spoken some version of that speech for at least five hours before I delivered it.

I also was given the chance to walk out onto the real stage, so that first step out there in prime time wouldn't be a complete shock.

I had delivered a speech at the 1984 convention and I had found that the audience pays attention to you when the lights are dimmed. When the hall lights are on they're more likely to be visiting with each other, watching the reporters, doing TV interviews, or making deals. When the lights are off, and the only light is coming from the stage, people will be more apt to listen to what you have to say. It's like putting a towel over a birdcage; they get quiet.

Gordon Wynne and I told the convention manager that I was not going to walk out onstage until they dimmed the lights. He wasn't happy to hear it. "I want to tell you," he said, "the networks are going to give us fits."

"I can't help it," I told him. "It's going to be a worse fit for you if I stop talking."

"Can't we raise the lights when the audience applauds?"

27

"You can use your judgment. But in general," I said, "I want the lights down. And if they don't go down and stay down, I'll just stop until they do."

Several weeks before, the convention planners had called to say that each speaker was to be introduced with a film before we spoke, and who would I like to narrate mine? I immediately said, "Willie Nelson," never dreaming that Willie would do it. They got in touch with him and he did it, and I really cherish that film.

There were all sorts of decisions to be made. What song did I want played when I walked to the podium? Jane chose "Deep in the Heart of Texas." Not "The Yellow Rose." Surely not.

The day of my last run-through, Mario Cuomo came down to the rehearsal room with his wife and son, and brought me a Steuben Glass apple. I may have seemed somewhat less than secure because he told me, "Ann, when I spoke I knew I was going to be a total bomb. Those people were not going to listen to me. And I just decided, what the heck, I would go ahead and I would go out there and say my piece, and if it wasn't any good I would still be the governor of New York."

Neal Spelce came up with another problem and another solution. He said that this speech, the words themselves, would be different from anything anyone had ever heard as a Keynote. I hadn't thought of it that way, because it was just so much me and the way I talk, but he was right. "We're going to have to prepare the press as best we can," he said, "for what they are going to hear."

I went looking for Walter Cronkite.

I had known Walter for a number of years, had been a guest speaker at a roast for him in Washington several years before. He had already called the hotel and said that if I got a chance I should come over and see him at the convention hall. He's a warrior in the media battle, and he can set the tone for an entire broadcast. If Walter, by treatment or inflection or posture, makes it clear that you're worth people's time, then your stock can just take off.

"Walter," I said when I found him, "I want you to be prepared for what kind of speech you're going to hear from me tonight." He looked at me. "I'm going to talk Texas."

He laughed. "Oh, well that's great."

Neal went around and talked to a number of press people about what to expect. They would be given copies of the speech before air time, and we knew that it wasn't going to be the same speech read as it was delivered. It was just not a reading speech, it was a delivery speech. A lot of speechwriters are writers first, not speechmakers, and they make the mistake of writing things that read beautifully but don't speak well. There's a real difference.

We got back to the hotel and I went to rest for a little while and listen to the *Chariots of Fire* soundtrack on my headphones. I had some very serious, prayerful talks with my higher power. Not to make the speech good, or to make me good, or to perform well, but to give me the strength to do this job. I tried to remind myself what was really important in my life. That no matter what happened, the two most important things in my life are my own self-respect and integrity and the love my children have for me. And I found that no matter what I did in that speech, I wouldn't lose my integrity or self-respect or the love of my children. It was a very liberating, calming thought.

When I got to the Omni I was numb. The kids were all done up in their new outfits and looked wonderful. Jane Hickie and Neal Spelce were in the background, at the door. Diane Sawyer had seen me in the rehearsal room and I had agreed that she would get to ask the first question when I got off the stage. You know, here you are, you're making the speech of your life, and you're trying to remember that when you leave you must talk to Diane Sawyer.

I walked out and there was applause, and the Texas delegation had these signs that were real cute that said, "Democrats ♥ Ann Richards." I'd seen cards and stickers and signs like that for athletes, states, and other politicians, but when you see signs with your own name on them it's pretty wonderful.

The Omni was a fabulous place to make a speech. There had been a lot of talk and complaining that it was too small for a convention of that size and magnitude, but for the speakers it was excellent. I was so close to the audience that I didn't feel removed from them. As big as the arena was, there was a certain intimacy to it. Michael Dukakis said it was like speaking in a Greek amphitheater, and it really was, because the audience was all the way around you.

I started, and immediately the audience was with me.

There's a real difference between delivering an address to a live crowd and speaking to millions of people on TV. Two entirely different techniques. There is one kind of speech, to a live audience, that gets them up on their feet, gets them enthusiastic, gets them shouting. That's a hot speech. There's a lot of emotion to it, a lot of passion. It comes from your gut. That kind of speech will not play well in your living room. You don't want people in your living room who are hot. You'll withdraw. You'll feel uncomfortable.

So from the start I was really worried about striking the balance in my delivery, so that it was hot enough for the 15,000 people in the auditorium but cool enough for the seventy million people in their living rooms.

The crowd loved the line about my accent. They loved the line about two women in 160 years being par for the course. They went crazy when Ginger Rogers danced backwards and in high heels.

I started to get real worried.

The audience was so up, so with it, so in sync with me and my speech that I was afraid I was too hot. I didn't want to cool down my delivery, but I didn't want to scald the home viewers.

And I worried a lot about eye contact. Neal Spelce had told me that being able to keep contact with the camera for living room delivery is really important. He also taught me that when there is applause, if there is applause, you can turn and look at one TelePrompTer and pick up the line that comes next, and then you can deliver it directly to the camera, right to the viewer. I was well enough rehearsed at that point that I could keep these technical things very much in my mind. I was speaking and thinking, speaking and thinking.

The audience was applauding more than we had planned. We had expected about ten or fifteen interruptions for laughs or applause. We ended up with forty-some-odd. We couldn't lose for winning.

Then I began to be concerned about the time. We had been allotted thirty minutes, applause included. I was definitely going to go over. Then I thought—mind you, I'm delivering the Keynote Address while all this thinking is going on—"If I go over, they're not going to cut me off. I'll just have to finish; there's no way to stop."

They had told me there would be a glass of water on the podium, and if there was applause—I had to keep telling myself, *when* there was applause—I could take a drink of water. (When you get nervous your mouth just cottons up. Some speakers put Vaseline on their lips, they get so dry.) Well, during one long round of applause I reached over to take a drink and my hand was shaking so badly that I slopped water all over the podium. I had to reach over and hold that glass with two hands to get it to my mouth. That's when I realized I was not as cool as I

31

thought I was. I thought, "Girl, that's the last bit of water you're going to get until this is over."

When I finished I really did not know how I'd done. When you're under that kind of tension, it's just hard to tell. I turned around and Paul Kirk was smiling, but people will always be kind to you the moment after. I hugged the children.

The audience was still applauding, so I knew I had to go back out and acknowledge that. By this time I was kind of comatose. A combination of adrenaline and psychological draining. I'd been pointing so hard toward that speech, those moments of delivery, that I had given no thought at all to what happens afterward.

Funny, the things you remember. I still had in mind that I had to go and say something to Diane Sawyer. She asked me, "How did you rate yourself?" And, as well as I can remember, I said, "Well, I really don't know. I was worried about my eye contact." That's the first thing that came to mind, and it was the exact truth.

Anne Wexler met me and said that Michael Dukakis was on the telephone and wanted to talk with me. I thought that was great. He said he liked the speech.

By now I was on cruise control. It would have taken a stampede of buffalo to put me into sharp focus. I did a series of pop-in interviews, the kind you see at all the conventions when the newspeople get a new face they don't know much about. I was feeling like a zombie, but I didn't look like one. I could be animated; I answered whatever anyone asked. With nothing to hide, and all these drafts of the speech in my head, anything I said would be okay. That's the joy of saying what you actually think in public; anything that comes out of your mouth is really yours. This seemed to surprise the anchors.

So I got hot in public. And my Mama was thrilled to death to meet the weatherman.

2

★

MY Daddy was born in a little community called Bugtussle. There are a lot of Bugtussles in Texas, in one place or another, but this one was outside of Lorena, just south of Waco.

Supposedly the community got its name because there was some fellow named Bug—could have been Bugg, for all I know—who caused a problem there. The town was the center of some kind of camp meeting, as they had in the rural South, where people would drive their buggies up and they would hear preaching and they would sing, and they would make a couple of days of it.

These people had children, and they would stack up brush and make a circle and bed these kids down on quilts—from whence came the expression "Baptist pallet"—and leave them in that circle while they went on about whatever their religious activity was.

It seems that while the children were asleep in their various buggies, Mr. Bug, who was a prankster, switched them from one buggy to another. After the ensuing melee, the town became known as Bugtussle.

I've always thought that was a pretty romantic and ridiculous story, and probably not true. But that's what my Daddy, Cecil, used to tell me.

My Daddy's Daddy was a farmer. Both my parents' folks were farmers. They came from places like Alabama and Tennessee, and they came to Texas like people did from all over the country, because it was a place of opportunity. They were looking for land to farm. In the late 1800s all across the South, there were letters scribbled on doors: "GTT." It meant "Gone to Texas."

My Mama, Iona Warren, was born outside of Hico, which is south of Fort Worth near Glenrose, in a community called Hogjaw. Honest to Pete. They both came from pretty big families, and really poor. Dirt poor. I think my father's pop left the farm and moved into Waco at some point, but my granddaddy on my mother's side, and my grandmother, lived on the Stephenville Highway until they both got too old to live out there and moved into town.

The family stayed close by. Sisters and brothers either lived with their parents even after they were grown and married or they built houses that were very near the home place.

My Mama was the adventurer. She finished what I think is the equivalent of high school and at some point decided to come to Waco. It must have been a very brave thing to do. Both her sisters stayed in Hico, still live there. But Mama was smart and she was ambitious.

It must have been frightening to leave a community where you had grown up, knew everybody, all your family was there, and go off on your own. My uncle I.V. was working in Waco and I guess he encouraged Mama to come. She didn't need much encouraging. She worked in a dry-goods store, selling piece goods and whatever else.

Daddy finished the eighth grade and it became a family necessity for him to go to work. All of the children in that family went to work very young. Even those who got to stay in school skeeted sodas or worked at a drive-in root-beer stand. This wasn't so they could have some spending change, it was so they could bring money home.

They were so poor that at one point the family had got a hold of a whole load of field tomatoes—either got them for nothing or got them for very little—and they peeled those tomatoes and cooked them, canned them, and ate them at every meal for months. My Daddy won't eat stewed tomatoes to this day.

Mama and Daddy met on a blind date. They went to a movie, but either the projector broke down or the film was damaged—anyway, they had to take a rain check, which meant that Daddy asked Mama out again.

When my parents married they bought a little one-bedroom frame house on an acre of land out on the Dallas Highway in Lakeview, about eight miles from Waco. It was just a little country community, didn't have a city council or any kind of government structure. It didn't even have a Main Street. You came into Lakeview off a couple of roads which connected to a highway. One of the roads had a country store and a filling station. There were the Interurban train tracks, which sooner or later led to Dallas, and across from them sat a tiny little grocery store. That was the total commerce of Lakeview.

It wasn't an ugly town, but it was not kept. There were empty lots, and fields where weeds grew. I don't know why in the world it would be called Lakeview; there was no lake to view.

Daddy was working for Southwestern Drug Company, driving a delivery truck, delivering pharmaceuticals and anything you could buy in a drugstore. At one point he had been making $100 a month, but when the Depression hit hardest his salary was reduced to $81.50.

The house cost $700 and my parents paid for it in two years. It seems inconceivable to me that anybody with a salary of $81.50 a month could pay off a mortgage like that so quickly, but they had a big garden and grew everything they ate. They raised chickens, the odd duck or goose, and at one point they had a hog. Everything was grown for food.

It was a little country house, with steps going up to a front porch and a white picket fence around it. There are lots of these frame houses up on hills off the roads of Texas. The main window is in the bedroom over the porch, and the living room always juts out with a big window there too. There are doors off the porch to each room. There's always a swing on the porch.

I was born in the bedroom of that house. Mama went into labor and someone had told her that if she would walk a lot she could make the baby come faster, so she spent most of the day walking up and down the dirt roads in Lakeview. Finally, in the evening, she called old Dr. Beidlespach to come on out from Waco.

I took my time in coming and there wasn't anything anybody could do about it. Dr. Beidlespach went and lay down on the front porch and slept there. He said if they made a bed for him he would never get up when the baby was ready.

I finally arrived at six the next morning.

Mama had gotten a neighbor woman to come in to cook supper for Daddy that night, but the neighbor woman couldn't kill the chicken that she was supposed to cook. My Daddy would be getting home any time now and something had to be done; there's no such thing as maternity leave when you're poor, not even for a moment. My Mama lay on the birthing bed, only hours after I was born, and wrung that chicken's neck so that Daddy would have supper when he got home.

I believe Mama would have liked to have had more children, but times were hard and I was the only one. Daddy had the fear—maybe that fear is indigenous to the Depression generation—that he wouldn't be able to afford all the things he wanted to give me, and he wanted to give me everything he'd never had. So they never had another child.

They were hard-working, thrifty people. My Mama was always trying to figure out how to make a little more money. Not that they were going to spend it on anything; any money we had either went into savings or toward necessities.

My parents never wanted me to have to work as hard as they did. But that was all I ever saw them do, and the message I got was that the only thing of any real value in life is hard work. It's strange the way things work out.

Mama never wanted me to be frivolous. I always had chores and she always had things for me to do. There were rules, and I was to be responsible. If I went to play with somebody in the neighborhood I could never stay longer than an hour. If I wasn't home by then, Mama would come after me. It always seemed like you just got started playing and you had to go home.

The wallpaper in my bedroom was full of bouquets. If you squinted your eyes just right you could make these little bou-quets march at an angle up and down the wall. If you pinched your eyes on each side you could make a triangle of bouquets. I remember trying to concoct that triangle and then trying to make those little bouquets march in and out of it.

The living room was a mystery. It was always dark in there. Mama had gone to Itasca, where they had a big mill, and bought yards and yards of gauzy fabric and made these really elaborate draperies which I thought were terribly exotic. There was a mohair couch and a mohair chair to match, and a coffee table. That coffee table was probably a late addition, but I feel sure we were the only people in Lakeview who had one. I was always puzzled why it would be called a coffee table; no one would ever dare put a cup of coffee on it.

About the only time anybody ever went in the living room was at Christmas or for a meeting of the Home Demonstration Club.

The Home Demonstration Club meeting was an event. Through the extension services of Texas A&M, there was a program in which an agent, usually a woman, would travel around rural communities and teach people how to do things: how to can, how to preserve food, how to quilt. I mean, there wasn't anywhere to go, and everyone would gather and sit around and wear their nicest clothes and listen to the Home Demonstration Lady tell them what new innovative thing was taking place in homemaking.

Mama had an ivy plant that she had trained, maybe tacked it up with some carpet tacks, so it snaked around and covered the whole wall of the porch like a maze. Probably the Home Demonstration Lady taught Mama that milk would make your ivy leaves shine, because one of my jobs was to polish the leaves of that ivy plant with milk. Every dusty leaf on that whole wall needed me and my bottle of milk's particular attention. Oh, I hated to do that job. I thought, "Who cares if those ivy leaves are dusty?!" Lord knows, I didn't.

When pressure cookers came out, we got one. They took a lot of the time out of cooking and made life a tiny bit simpler. There was a little black rubber release valve on the top of the cooker, about the size of a dime. Well, one afternoon I guess my Mama had put on a pot of beans and walked over to the henhouse, when World War II came to our door.

They had built an Army Air Force base right near our little town and there was a lot of talk at school about the wisdom of living near something like that; we were all virtually certain that we were prime targets of the Japanese. Lakeview was in the bombsights and there was a tremendous explosion in our kitchen.

I was absolutely terrified. The Japanese were right overhead! It sounded like Iwo Jima!

What had happened was that the release valve to the pressure cooker had blown off like a mortar and these hard little beans began to blow out of the hole rapidfire and hit the kitchen ceiling.

Well, I didn't know that. I knew we were under attack, the Japanese had found us at last. I ran to the one place in our house that was sanctuary, the place not even the Japanese would dare enter: the living room. I ran in there, hid behind that mohair chair, and wet my pants!

The Home Demonstration Club didn't always bring disaster. They taught sewing and brought patterns. My mother was a skilled seamstress; she made all my clothes. A lot of us wore dresses made out of feed sacks, and in the really old days they said Bewley Mills on them, which was a big flour mill. Everything came in sacks—flour, sugar, feed—so we'd get fed and get a wardrobe at the same time. Then the fabric manufacturers got smart and started making feed sacks with designs on them, little flowers and such.

I always got to play the lead roles in the school plays, or be leader of the rhythm band, because my mother would make the costumes for me. There weren't many women who knew how to do that. I liked stepping out in front, and Mama would buy me the boots with the tassels hanging on the front. No telling how dear those boots were, but she got them.

The Home Demonstration Club was for the women. The men had their own circle. My Daddy, along with our neighbors Boots Douglas and Aubrey Rogers, built what they called a pavilion. I guess we would call it a gazebo today, but to them it was The Pavilion. It had wooden sides about four or five feet high and was screened in above that, and it was just big enough for a domino table. Somewhere Daddy had picked up a slab of marble and they built some kind of base for it, but truthfully, I suspect that the games went on out there because there was not a room in anybody's house that was big enough to play dominoes. (They could have played it on our dining room table, but that was reserved for much more special occasions.)

The men used to sit in the Pavilion and play dominoes and the women would sit around and talk. I was supposed to go to bed, but there was kind of a porch off the kitchen that looked out over the back yard to the Pavilion and I can remember sneaking out of bed and going and listening to the stories being told and all the men laughing.

My Daddy was then and is now a great storyteller. He was six feet four and a handsome man, and he'd tell these bawdy, raunchy tales. But they were always so funny because of the way Daddy would tell them—he was so gleeful about it! He was so excited when he had a new story to tell. When he started he would back up, like he needed plenty of room to laugh, and he would do this little yarn-spinning dance, take two or three steps backward as he would get into the telling, and as he came to the punchline he would bend over and just laugh all over you. Well, even if the story wasn't funny you would laugh because Daddy's laugh was so infectious.

A lot of the things we did for fun were in dead earnest, to get food. If we took an outing and went fishing, it wasn't some kind of sport. You were out there getting fish—to eat. We would set trotlines from one side of the river to the other; at various points we would put a line and hook in place along it, bait the hook, and pray that some big old catfish would come along and like whatever we'd offered.

My Daddy used blood bait. You might be able to buy it at a bait stand, but I can't imagine Daddy buying anything that cost any money. More likely he got it somewhere where they slaughtered animals. Blood bait was just coagulated blood; felt like Jell-O, and the greatest honor in the world would be when my Daddy said, "Hand me a pinch of that blood bait." It was like being cabin boy to the captain of a ship.

You try to run trotlines late at night before you go to bed, and it was always eerie and mysterious. It was dark by the river and you'd have to carry a lantern in the boat as you paddled along the line, pulling the hooks out of the water one by one to bait them. We were forever spooked about snakes. Water moccasins. I don't know whether we thought they were going to jump up into the boat or what, but it was real quiet down there and we were mighty careful.

Snake stories abounded. Once we were staying at a cabin on the Bosque River owned by a family named Whicker, and I was admiring their ingenuity. They had wrapped what looked like a snakeskin around an electric wire and it sure did make a striking impression above the door. I reached up to scratch it and the thing crawled off. Scared the squat out of me.

We went hunting and sometimes we had hunting dogs. There are probably a million hunting-dog stories about how "We had that ol' dog in the back of the truck, and somehow we drove up to the gas station and the dog wasn't in there, and there we were 175 miles from home. And we got home and three days later . . . here comes ol' Rosie." Well, we had one of those stories about one of Daddy's dogs.

If we got an opportunity to go on somebody's deer lease or somebody's farm and kill a deer—that was absolutely wonderful. You could make sausage out of it, you could cure the whole thing and eat for months. It was a great treat.

I loved to go visit my mother's family in Hico. It would be summertime and I would get to ride the Dinky. The Dinky was a small train with an engine that had four or five black and white stripes on it. Chevrons. Looked like a locomotive with four or five mustaches. Some of the boys used to put pennies on the track, that was a big deal. We used to run behind the Dinky and yell, "Freezie, Freezie!" The story was that the engineer would throw used flares to you if you did that, but he never did.

My mother's sisters, my aunts Elta and Oleta, lived in Hico, and they just loved me to death. I don't believe I've been anywhere in my life where I've felt so loved as I did when I was in Hico.

My grandmother and granddaddy loved me too. Granddaddy was a big, big man, somewhere around 250 pounds. They lived out in the country and didn't have electricity until they were in their early seventies, but this was well before then.

My granddaddy was a tough taskmaster; the men were in his time. He would whip those kids with a razor strop and they were afraid of him. He was also a drinker. One time I found all his empty whiskey bottles out in the barn and broke every last one of them. I don't know why. Hico was dry, and if you got anything to drink it wasn't easy to come by.

But my granddaddy was wonderful to me. He could tell stories endlessly, and the kids would just sit around him in rapture. He would tell stories about this critter that came through the country and would kill every farm animal on your place. And this critter, he'd tell us, only left one track. Now that takes some thinking about, right? Nobody'd seen it, nobody ever caught it, but they would wake up one morning and all the hogs, all the cows, everything in the barnyard would be stone dead. And this critter just left one track.

My granddaddy let it be known that this critter was still out there on the loose. And, he said, we never know when it will break out and start eating children too.

There was a woman who had a place on the other side of my granddaddy's and he told us that she was so fancy that she had a fan in her outhouse. It wasn't inside the outhouse, it was behind the house—so when she sat down on that hole there would be this cool, cool breeze blowing on her!

And, of course, we'd believe everything he said.

Grandmama and Granddaddy had a storm cellar, just a mound of dirt with a vent pipe stuck in it and a door on it. They had just gone underground and hollowed out a hole, put some stone pavers down on the dirt to form steps going down into it, built some shelves and had themselves a cooling house. They kept smoked meats and canned goods down there.

There was nothing worse than being sent to the storm cellar. You'd be told to go out there and get a jar of peaches or something, and you didn't really want to go. It smelled like a cavern, that musty, mildewy underground smell like you yourself were about to be planted.

And just as you'd get to the door my granddaddy would holler, "Watch out for snakes!" Never failed.

I always thought my grandmama was frail, but she must have been as hardy as an ox. She was all the time cooking for everyone. There were always hot biscuits, two or three different kinds of vegetables, collards and beans; it was always a spread.

The men ate first. Coming in from the fields, definitely, but even if it was a special occasion. We would drive up on Christmas Day and when it came time for the chicken dinner, the men always ate first and the women served. And then, after the men were finished, the women and children ate. But, of course, by the time the men got through there wasn't anything left but wings and necks and gizzards. It would not have occurred to anyone to do anything differently, or to leave something over. The men would eat just what they wanted to eat. And it certainly would not have occurred to the women that it should be done any other way.

Another reason for going to Hico in the summer was for very serious business: I had to get a permanent.

My hair has always been a source of some embarrassment. My Daddy's mother, who I called Nanny, had real thin hair and so did my Daddy's sisters. My Mama had thick, wavy, naturally curly hair, really nice hair. I was a very thin, skinny, scrawny child with thin, skinny, scrawny hair, and Mama always said I had "Willis hair." So in the summer I would go to Hico and a woman named Carmen would give me a permanent.

It probably cost three dollars, and it was one of those big

machines where you sat under it and they put these rollers in your head and poured all this crimping solution on it, and then they hooked you up to these heated covers that fit over the rollers and were connected to electrical wires that ran up into a central unit.

It would kind of burn my hair into a squiggly nest and I'd have to live with it. My modified Willis hair would be very tight and unattractive for the first month or two, and then just sort of hang limp the rest of the time. Mama would roll my hair up so that it would "look nice," and then put a hair net on it—not one of those real-hair hair nets like old ladies wear, but one of those heavy hair nets—and then send me off to school.

The net was to keep the hair nice, but no one could see my hair under it. I decided that was foolish. I would take it off before I got to school and put it back on when I was walking down the road on the way home.

When Toni home permanents came out, that was a great breakthrough. Mama said no self-respecting woman would have straight hair once they'd invented Toni home permanents.

I was always taking lessons. Whatever it was that they had to offer, Mama wanted to make sure I took it. If she had anything to say about it, I was going to learn something else besides hard work. I would ride five miles on my bicycle over to Mrs. Glenn's house for piano lessons, and there was a woman who would drive out from Waco to our schoolhouse and teach Expression.

Expression meant you had to memorize some little ditties and poems and then get up and say them at a recital. I was really good at that. I would cut out stories from whatever I could find and paste them in my little book, and then at recital I would shine. I was nothing but a little-bitty first-grader but I was taught early to stand up and say my piece.

My best friend was a girl named Regina Garrett. She had

bright red hair and everybody called her Rusty. She was real cute and short and, I thought, popular. I was always kind of weeny, wimpy, and skinny. Mama would follow me around with cod liver oil and everything else in the world, trying to get me to eat.

Lakeview had one paved road. Everybody's mailbox stood on it, but the road to each house was dirt. When Rusty and I would go see each other and play I was allowed to walk only as far as our mailbox with her, then I'd have to turn for home. At my road she and I would walk backwards, waving to each other until we got out of sight.

Across the road from our house was an open field with some oaks, but what I remember best are the chinaberry trees. There was a big one in our backyard. Chinaberry trees are short-lived and brittle; the limbs fall off in the rain. But they bloom a beautiful cluster of amethyst-colored blossoms with a sweet, sweet smell to them. In spring and summer the trees are full of bees, and the smell of chinaberry is everywhere. The blossoms turn into little hard round green berries, which then fall off and turn into squishy yellow berries. We had regular chinaberry wars and chucked the berries at each other.

My other friend was Virginia Lynn Douglas. Virginia Lynn lived across the street from me in her parents' house, which was right next door to her grandmama's and granddaddy's house. I think the Douglases had less money than we did.

They were always reading at the Douglases'. They had all the Nancy Drew books. Virginia Lynn had read the Bible, and her father, Boots, gave her a dollar when she did. I thought that was really remarkable, first that she could read it and second that he would give her a dollar to do it. I had one book growing up: *Heidi.* It's an okay book, but it's not the whole literary world.

Daddy read the *Saturday Evening Post* and the newspaper, and I would borrow books from Virginia Lynn, but growing up reading makes a lot of difference in the appetite you have for it. Mama was a little impatient when I wanted to read. I think she thought it was a good thing to do in the abstract, but that when it got right down to it, really, it took you away from your work if you were just reading a book. Perhaps it was the denial of books then that makes me such an avid reader now.

I was always the youngest in my class at school. All twelve grades were in one building and I never had more than fifteen kids in my whole grade. My folks didn't really care about my grades—scholarship was not something that mattered all that much to them—but they wanted me to go to college and get an education "just in case."

There wasn't much doing in school. It was just school. I talked out in class a lot and probably drove everybody crazy. I remember many more times than once hearing, "Dorothy Ann, if you don't quit talking . . ." (My name was Dorothy Ann Willis. I dropped the Dorothy in high school.)

I loved the plays at school and I wanted to be in every one. I could never carry a tune, so I couldn't be in any of the musicals, and I remember one time we put on a show about Texas history and there were three or four kids who got to dress up like cowboys and sit around the red cellophane fake fire and sing "Cool Water." I wasn't one of them and I was so envious.

The PTA had raised a considerable amount of money to put an intercom system into the school building, the idea being to open each school day with the news of the moment and a prayer. But it was also used for other purposes. Kids were forever getting into trouble, as kids will, and the principal, Mr. Grady Moore, had the brilliant idea to begin Radio Discipline. When a boy needed to be reprimanded for some form of unacceptable behavior, Mr. Moore would flip the PA switch in the principal's office and say, "The voice you are about the hear is Charles Goodall." Everybody in the school would listen and, after a *rap* with a ruler, this poor kid would begin to holler.

I don't quite know how it happened, but my Daddy became a member of the school board and created quite a stir. It seems that a fourth-grade teacher, Mrs. Julian, became pregnant and many members of the board weren't going to let her continue at her job because it wouldn't be seemly for anyone who "showed" to teach school to the community's impressionable children.

My father got up and said that that was the most ridiculous thing he'd ever heard. This woman was married to a man who was in the service, and she was literally depending on that income for her livelihood. My Daddy was never a firebrand progressive—far from it—but that was pretty amazing. And the board listened to him. He saved her job and she taught school that year.

The church was the center of all religious and social happenings in Lakeview. There was a Baptist church in town and a Church of Christ, but we were Methodists.

It was nothing romantic—no stained glass, no artifacts, no relics. Not even Sheetrock. Just whitewashed boards all around and a bare elevated pulpit. There was a low railing up in front, and when you joined the church, or when you were called to Jesus, you would walk up the center aisle to that wood railing.

This was a very poor church. The most valuable item that church owned was a Shirley Temple cup. It was smoky blue glassware and had Shirley Temple's face and her signature in white across the front of it. That's what they used to baptize you with. Later on, a man with some woodworking skills joined the church and he made a pedestal and a wooden bowl for that purpose, much more uptown-looking, but for the longest time you were introduced to the Lord by Shirley Temple.

It was quiet inside and the floorboards creaked when you walked on them each Sunday. A wooden plaque with removable numbers hung on the wall, telling the number of people in attendance at Sunday school that Sunday, the total number of community church members, and how many people had showed up for church the week before. There weren't many, maybe sixty.

If you went to Sunday school religiously every Sunday you got a sheep to paste on your Jesus picture.

We each had this 8 × 10 picture portrait of Jesus sitting on a stone in the middle of a meadow. One by one you could paste these little sheep on it, and I thought that was wonderful. I wanted the whole flock.

On special occasions there would be a covered-dish event held on the grounds outside the church. We saw this more as getting together with your neighbors than getting next to the Almighty, although I suspect the gatherings were organized to increase interest in the church. I remember my Mama and I cooked a lot of stuff and took it places. There was no such thing as going to someone's house for dinner; people didn't do that. Either you went to an event or you went on a picnic where everybody brought something.

I could never sing in front of people in school, but I could sing with everybody else in the choir and I had a great time at it.

My friend Regina and I used to sit in church and play this game, "Between the Sheets." I'm sure this was after we got much older and much more sophisticated—about ten or eleven. We would read the titles of the hymns and then say, "between the sheets."

"Just As I Am" ("between the sheets").

"Love Lifted Me" ("between the sheets").

And, of course, we'd get real tickled and sit there in church and snicker.

At that time, the preachers who were sent to those little country churches were either older men who had been rejected somewhere else or young men just out of theology seminary and just learning. We got this minister, I think his name was Reverend Craig, and he was into the Holy Ghost. He would preach hellfire and damnation and he would jingle the coins or keys in his pocket, and he got it going pretty good.

There were two sisters in the congregation, the Freeman girls, who were always seized with the Holy Spirit. (That's country language, "the Freeman girls." If people ask about them it would always be "Now let me see, the Freeman girls. Didn't one of them marry the Jones boy?" I was "that Willis girl.")

The Freeman girls' eyes would roll back in their heads and they would get real stiff, they would fall down on the floor and their tongues would hang out of their mouths and they would moan and carry on, and it was really awesome. I'd sit there and watch them, and so would everyone else. The Sunday service became a real show and these two women were monopolizing it.

My Daddy was on the church's board of stewards, and he was extremely impatient with this kind of carrying on. It's one thing to bring people to the light, it's quite another to daze them with it. Daddy thought that this guy was just going a little too far.

There was a big blowout over it. Part of the community was offended by the holy rolling, another part by my Daddy. My Daddy got offended by the whole thing; he resigned from the board and never went back to church. Mama and I went, but Daddy stayed away.

There were lots of events that went on at the church. They may have had Home Demonstration meetings there too. There was always an Easter egg hunt. One year it was held in the lot to the side of the church and all the congregation's children were there.

The prize egg that year, not just any colored egg but the

one that if you found it would make you the year's real winner, was made out of crystallized sugar. They showed it around before they hid it and you could look in a little hole at one end and see all kinds of little colors and patterns inside. I wanted it real bad. The elders hid the eggs while we all shuffled and shifted in our Easter finery, and then they let the kids loose.

Where could that egg be? I wasn't much interested in any of the others, I wanted that crystalline sugar egg.

I saw it! Partly hidden halfway up a window ledge, it was perched for the taking. No one else saw it but me! I didn't think of slowly ambling over and picking it off. I made a run for it.

I was running across the church yard when one of the mothers looked at me, looked at my destination . . . and spotted the egg. She called her daughter's name and pointed. The little girl started shouting. She was screaming. "There it is! There it is! I see the Easter egg. I've got it! It's mine!"

Everybody turned around. First they heard her screaming, then they saw me running.

She got the egg.

I clawed and cried and pitched such an almighty fit that my Mama had to take me home. The unfairness of it! I saw it first. Mothers aren't even supposed to be there; it's not their Easter egg hunt, it's ours. That girl never even touched it. She would never have seen it if I hadn't seen it first. She knew that. Her mother knew that. But neither of them said a word. They just took my crystallized sugar egg. I was shouting and struggling and gulping for air all the way home. I believe that was the first time I was really made to see that life is not necessarily fair, that honor does not always triumph, not even in church, and that I shouldn't expect it to.

I had school shoes, but I only wore them in school. You always took your shoes off, and you didn't have to wait until you got home to do it, because the more you wore them the more you wore them out. The roads in Lakeview were like hot dust in the summer and the first few days you'd be moving around real quick, but after the first couple of weeks your feet would toughen up so you could take it.

I did a lot of walking around barefoot. Well, actually, I can't remember ever walking; I ran everywhere. I fell down a lot; my knees and shins were always scabby. My Daddy said I was a perpetual motion machine, always squirming around like a worm in hot ashes.

I hated naps. Hated them. When I was too young for school, or during the summers, my Mama would make me go in and lie down for a while. I don't know whether she wanted to take a nap herself, or if she was worried that I'd just go *boing* one day like a broken spring, but she did build this midday nap into my routine. I would lie there just as long as I could with my eyes wide open, determined not to blink because if I blinked I might go out. It seemed like such a waste of time.

But I *was* always getting into something. Rusty and I used to smoke cedar bark. You take the bark from a cedar post, strip it, crumble it, shred it, and roll it up in paper. If you could get cigarette paper, that was very exotic; I don't ever remember having any. No, these were stogie-sized operations. The major problem was sneaking the matches to be able to light these things. One time when we did, Rusty and I built a little fire up near Rusty's house and we set the woods on fire. We had to call her granny to come put it out.

I climbed trees. When *Superwoman* comics came out I really believed that I could be her. I got on the roof of the garage with a rope—a magic lariat—and jumped off. I believed I could do anything, and my father encouraged me to believe it. Mama did too, with the caveat that you just had to work at it.

And when you work at it, she told me, you have to do the job right. If I had a chore or task and I didn't do it perfectly, I had to go back and do it again.

Oh, how I hated that. When I shined those ivy leaves, if I missed some I had to go back and do it *all* over again. If I missed a little crumb clinging to the side of the skillet I had to go back and rewash the whole skillet. When I learned to iron, if I didn't iron a blouse right I had to sprinkle it down and go back and iron it again. Mama taught me to sew, and if the stripes didn't match exactly on a seam, well then you had to tear it out and sew it over. It had to be quality or it really wasn't worth anything. You had to be sure that you did it right, and did it right the first time—because that would eat into whatever time you had to play.

I don't want to paint a portrait here that I was some poor little kid who worked all the time. There probably was no child in this world more loved than I was. Mama and Daddy expected something of me, they just didn't know quite what.

There wasn't a whole lot going on around my house. We had a telephone, but there weren't a great number of places to call. And besides, it was a party line; you never knew who might be listening in. One of our neighbors was Miss Lucas, who was known as "Telephone, Telegraph, Tell-A-Lucas," because anything Miss Lucas picked up you could be sure the whole community was going to know.

Up the road a ways there was a man who bred and raised greyhounds. Of course, betting was against the law in Texas, but there were these backwoods events where they would race these dogs, and it was pretty big-time stuff. Dogs are important in Texas.

My Mama hated those greyhounds. They would come down and suck her eggs.

Those dogs would break into her henhouse. First she'd have to worry about them killing the chickens, but if they didn't do that, then they would bite the end out of all the eggs and suck the whites and yolks out of them.

That's right, exactly. People think those expressions are made up. Egg-sucking dogs.

One time when those dogs got into the henhouse, Mama and I scalded those chickens in the washing machine. If you get to the birds quickly enough you can still eat them, and we didn't have enough food to be throwing away chickens. Mama usually scalded them one at a time in an iron pot and then plucked them, but this one time I swear she ran the hot water and threw the whole mess of them into the washer.

If my Mama and Daddy didn't put a lot of stock in scholarship, they greatly valued personality. I was always encouraged to perform, not just by my folks but by the Whickers and the Rogerses, people who were our friends in the neighborhood. I learned early on that people liked you if you told stories, if you made them laugh. People loved my Daddy.

I was nine years old the first time I saw my father cry. World War II had been claiming the local men—a lot of Lakeview's boys were going away and not coming home— and Daddy got drafted into the Navy. Townspeople hung little stars in their windows to serve notice that they had a child in the service, but I was virtually untouched by all that, with the exception of being afraid of the Japanese bombing us. But the night before he left, we were in the back room and my father hugged me and broke down and cried. We were not a touching family, we didn't do a lot of embracing, so I remember the moment when he reached for me as if it were this morning.

Daddy was thirty-five when he was drafted. A month later they stopped drafting men with children. He went through boot camp and pharmaceutical school, and was stationed in San Diego. Mama and I were on our own but she was a resourceful woman. Even before Daddy got drafted she had gone to comptometer school at 4C Business College so that when he did have to go into the military she would have a skill and a way to earn some money.

Mama was a real worker. She got a job at Southwestern Drug, where Daddy had worked, in what was called the sample room, which was glorious. It was filled with toasters and music boxes and toys and all the things people bought as gifts at drugstores, and we could buy things wholesale.

I don't remember too much about the time without Daddy, not even how long it was. I do know that at some point we moved out to be with him.

We drove.

This was a big adventure, not the kind of thing a woman was supposed to do with any degree of safety or sanity. Mama killed all the chickens and canned them because she knew that things were going to cost a lot in San Diego. We filled the car with canned goods and all of our belongings, strapped Mama's sewing machine into the trunk, gathered a second cousin, Fannabee Fryer, and lit out for California.

Daddy says when we got there we looked like the Joads, straight out of *The Grapes of Wrath*.

It was wartime and housing in San Diego was so scarce that we lived in one room underneath someone's house. I slept on a cot and the place was so small I had to get up so that Daddy could get out the door in the morning.

Eventually we found an apartment. My parents were scandalized at the thirty dollars a month we had to pay, and my Daddy didn't live there all the time. He lived at the naval base during the week and would come home on the weekends.

There was no demand for my Mama's comptometer skills, and we needed money. I hand-lettered a sign that said "Alterations and Dressmaking," and we put it in front of our apartment at the corner of Avenue A and Hawthorne, and Mama started taking in sewing.

My mother got very sick in California. She had an ectopic pregnancy and was bleeding a lot. The doctors kept telling her that she was going through an early change of life, but later they had to rush her to the hospital. I didn't understand any of this at the time; all I knew was that when she came home she was in bed for a while and I had to be careful, I could upset Mama easily.

But living in San Diego was like looking through binoculars for me. I had grown up in this tiny, tiny place and suddenly the world just opened up. I ate my first doughnut.

I had never even seen a doughnut. There were no doughnut shops in Lakeview, and not one deep-fat fryer. Mama baked pies and cakes and biscuits and bread, but doughnuts were a whole new heaven. Doughnut holes especially; I thought they were the greatest things in the world and they cost about three cents.

Mama would send me to this grocery store half a block down the street, which was another shock. Remember, we grew almost everything we ate in Lakeview and all of a sudden we had a grocery store nearby. I would get whatever it was she sent me for and I would take three pennies out of her purse and buy a doughnut hole. I had to gobble down the whole thing before I got home so she wouldn't know I'd done it.

I went to school at Theodore Roosevelt Junior High School, way across town. I'd walk about a block to the bus stop and ride the bus to central San Diego, then change and catch a streetcar that would take me to school. The streetcar went across a high trestle through Balboa Park and you could see a long way down either side and it seemed like a forest.

I thought my school was really pretty. Spanish architecture, tile roofs—it looked like something out of the movies. It was nothing like Lakeview. Neither were my classmates.

This was my first exposure to kids who were Italian and Greek and black and Hispanic. It was a real eye-opener. I can still remember some of their names; Helen Castenada, Josephine Giacalone.

Occasionally I would go to their houses, but it was rare. This was not a neighborhood school; kids came from all over San Diego, and my folks were probably justifiably concerned about me getting around in a big city. I was all of eleven years old and this was a city full of thousands of young sailors and Marines, and God knows they must be wild, or I guess that's what my parents thought.

Going to California at that time was like going to a foreign country. There were kids of different colors who came from different backgrounds but who were just like me. I was never able to understand racial prejudice after that.

There were no blacks living in Lakeview and you'd only see a black person once in a while; they'd come by the house and offer to do day labor, but they didn't live anywhere nearby. There were blacks in Waco, but they lived in East Waco. They had their own high school; there was never any mixing. You would see black people in Waco down on the square.

There was racial prejudice everywhere when I was growing up. Texas was a totally segregated state. About the only black person I met before I went to California was a man named Smoke Munson who worked with my Daddy at Southwestern Drug. The company had a picnic every year and they barbecued vast quantities of chicken and beef, and my Daddy and Smoke Munson did most of the barbecuing. When I would visit Daddy at the loading dock where he and Smoke worked, Smoke would lift me up and they would put me on the scale where they weighed the packages, and he would brag about how big I was. My Daddy would always laugh with him and I had the sense that they were great friends.

But there was no question that the general attitude was that blacks were inferior to whites. Blacks, of course, had been forced so long into the most menial, low-paying, low-skilled jobs. Black women rarely had an opportunity to work at anything but cleaning or washing and ironing. In Texas and all over the South, that's the way things worked.

I can remember hearing the expression, "He's a good nigger." Or, "He's one Jew that will give you the shirt off his back," meaning unlike the others. Prejudice is rarely individual, it's always universal. Smoke Munson was a wonderful man, but unfortunately he would have been described as "the exception that proved the rule."

It all stemmed from ignorance, unfamiliarity, and a need to feel superior at the expense of others. It's an unthinking, unreasoned emotional reaction: "I must be okay because there is another whole group of people that I consider inferior to me." Prejudice is such a strange and pathetic form of elevating oneself.

Eleanor Roosevelt came to the Naval Hospital while we were in San Diego and refused to allow her photograph to be made unless there was a "colored man" in the picture. Well, that occupied a lot of conversation, let me tell you. I thought she was bold and exciting. She must have been a remarkable woman.

The war ended, and after twenty-two months in the service my Daddy was discharged and we went back to Texas.

I played basketball for the Lakeview Bulldogs. In rural, small-town Texas the competition between schools is really intense. There is very little in terms of entertainment and things that kids can do, so these sports events are a very big thing. I was always so skinny and scrawny that I was not much of a basketball player, but I did get to play. It was particularly ludicrous because a lot of who we played against were these big old strong country girls. I mean, they were stout.

In those days, girls were not allowed to play full court. You either played offense or defense, you weren't allowed to cross the mid-court line, and you weren't allowed to dribble the ball more than three times in a row. The game, like our lives, was pretty restricted.

We had these little uniforms which our parents had saved dearly to buy for us, and I thought I looked pretty good. There was a boy I knew who went to school at Ross, a little town up near West, Texas, and Abbot (Willie Nelson's hometown), and I knew he was at the game. I had a free throw coming, and just as I was about to take my shot this voiced boomed out from high up in the bleachers. It was that boy from Ross, and he hollered really loud and clear, "Make that basket, birdlegs!"

I really do feel that most people see themselves much as they did when they were very young. Whatever the world thought of them when they were young kids, they pretty much think of themselves that way now. I certainly do. In my mind's eye I'm probably still that skinny kid trying to make that basket.

I graduated from Lakeview in whatever fashion one graduates from junior high, and, because Mama and Daddy felt that I needed to have a first-class education, we moved into Waco. It must also have been that after they had gone to California, their world had opened up too.

We rented a very small place out on Beverly Drive and Mama began the business of building us a house.

Mama and Mr. Whicker drew up plans for her dream house, she and Daddy bought a parcel of land on North 35th Street, and she started putting it up.

A house costs money, and I'm sure Mama had saved it from every single thing she and Daddy ever did. I mean, it was Waste not, want not, Wear it out and wear it again. She had been putting aside money from Daddy's wages and her sewing. In Waco Daddy had gone back to Southwestern Drug and progressed from delivery driver to salesman, and was probably one of their best.

And I promise you that Mama built that house for half what it would have cost anyone else. She would drive down to the unemployment office, or to the square where men were hanging out, and she'd name a price and say, "Do you want to work?" Then she would take a carload of men out to the job site.

That house was no small deal. It had two bedrooms at one end, then a den with a fireplace, a living room with another fireplace and a big picture window, a formal dining room, a kitchen, and what was called a breezeway connecting to a double garage with an Austin stone exterior and a big cement patio in the back with a barbecue pit that Daddy used every weekend. It was really a remarkable undertaking.

Somewhere Mama had found a houseful of accessories—mantels and doors, copper doorknobs and door plates, and all kinds of things from some old house—and I spent hours cleaning them before they were installed in our new house. Mama did a lot of the painting herself.

I spent a lot of time alone that year, more time than I was accustomed to, while she was building that house. I would come home from school and she would not be there, and when she and Daddy would come home they'd both be real tired.

As Mama started her house, I started at Waco High School. I was determined to be a new person.

I wanted to be "somebody," and high school was that new beginning where I could prove somehow that I was worth something and that people should like me. Mama and Daddy had high expectations, but exactly what they were neither they nor I knew. I just knew that my standards were way beyond me. Way beyond me. It seems like I was scared all the time.

I guess that I felt that the old me was kind of pathetic and inadequate. I was always afraid I wasn't measuring up. I never thought I was smart enough, I knew I wasn't pretty enough, and whenever I succeeded I thought it was a mistake. When you live like that, you always feel like you're faking it; like sooner or later they will all catch on and that will be the end of you.

The first thing I did was change my name. Dorothy Ann Willis, to me, meant a kind of country girl who couldn't compete in this new big-city sophisticated milieu. I dropped my first name and registered as Ann. And I did not tell my parents that I was going to do it.

My first day, all the freshmen were in study hall going through orientation and I walked around and introduced myself to all these total strangers. No one else did it; it must have been perfectly ridiculous. Rusty had moved to Waco and she was there that morning. I went up to her and laughingly said, "Hi, I'm Ann Willis." She looked up at me and said icily, "How old did you say you are?" It laid me to waste.

Mama was pleased that I was going to Waco High School for another reason: she hoped I would get to know a group of kids who weren't poor. I don't think she cared about me being rich, she just cared about me not being poor. In Lakeview we had probably been as well off as anybody in the community. But in Waco we were definitely not as well off as a lot of the kids with whom I went to high school.

I never thought of us as poor, but in high school I became much more aware of what it took to provide all the accouterments of a higher level of living. Waco was very much a traditional Southern city in terms of its societal structure; there were definitely the Haves and the Have Nots. I'll never forget the first cashmere sweaters I owned. We bought most clothes on sale and then would put them up for next year; we would put a down payment on them and then Mama would pay them out.

Mama knew what I ought to wear. She was still sewing most of my clothes. Most of the other kids had store-bought clothes, but I never minded wearing what Mama made; she made beautiful clothes.

In high school we all had to take the Kuder Preference Test. It asked things like, "Would you rather watch a TV, fix a TV, or sell a TV?" and was supposed to direct you towards a likely profession. I always tested higher in careers with a predilection toward being with people. People skills. I don't think I ever placed any value in that, as if *I* did it well so it must not be worth much. That's what I carried around with me.

I wasn't much of a student. Anything that I was interested in I could do pretty well, but anything that didn't catch my fancy I simply let go. Math was really difficult for me. I think I nearly flunked trigonometry. But I loved my English classes and I did really well in speech. I liked any class where I got to talk a lot.

The new me always wanted to do everything. If somebody was going to call the roll, I wanted to do it. If somebody was going to pass the paper out, well, I wanted to do that. I had so much energy that sitting still was painful. Do not forget that you are dealing here with a worm in hot ashes.

The best thing that happened in my freshman year was Mattie Bess Coffield's speech class. The class was more than just speech, it was debate. I'm a logical thinker, and that is really what debating is all about. The verbal, oral expression is important, and that's what I did well. We debated both sides of an issue and I had to be sure what my thesis was and be able to make logical arguments for the side I was on.

In Miss Coffield's class I competed in extemporaneous speech, declamation, debate, and acted in one-act and three-act plays. I'd always been able to talk; now I was getting good grades for it.

I liked the idea of competing with other schools. And it was a good excuse to get out of class; if you were in interscholastic league competition you could always get a pink slip to go to Miss Coffield's room to work on something or other, or to the library and avoid whatever studying you were supposed to be doing.

It never occurred to me not to debate. I loved it. My Daddy encouraged me, and I believe it was the first thing I did where Mama really rewarded me. If I went to a speech tournament and we won, I would come home and Mama would cook macaroni and cheese, my favorite. It was her way of saying, "We are glad that you won, and you did a good job."

But debating wasn't the only thing I was introduced to my freshman year. I had my first date that winter.

I was probably fourteen and my parents wouldn't let me have dates. I was always younger than my classmates and I think Mama felt that I would "grow up too fast." Most kids began going to the show together in junior high school, and by the ninth grade girls were wearing their boyfriend's ring on a chain. No girl who wanted to be popular was a freshman in high school before she had her first date. So I had a gap in that boyfriend/girlfriend period in which I just didn't learn the skills.

I was befriended by a girl named Janey Baker. Janey had a car. Her parents were divorced and she was allowed to do all kinds of things. I had been asked to a dance and Janey convinced my mother to let me go.

It was a DeMolay Dance (DeMolay is a junior group of the Masons) and I needed a formal dress in a hurry. My mother knew someone who had a dress that would fit me, so I borrowed the dress, got a pair of thong summer sandals, wore my Aunt Juanita's big fur coat—which was totally inappropriate for a fourteen-year-old girl to wear anywhere—and went to the ball.

Well, I didn't know how to dance. It was my first date, I was a nervous wreck, and the poor guy who asked me was not much better. And what made it worse was that we were double-dating with one of the most beautiful girls in the school.

We got in line for punch. Remember, I was going to be new and likable and popular . . . and I threw up all over the girl in front of me, my date, the borrowed dress, and the marble floor.

We loaded into the car to go home and the boy in the backseat lit up a cigarette. There was this terrible buildup of smoke and throw-up all over my clothes, and there was no-where to hide. I felt certain that my life was over.

I had a friend I liked a lot whose name was J. B. Little. J. B. had grown up with the Haves, but he didn't have a car, so he was on the outer fringes of Waco High School society. I always felt behind the rest of the kids in knowing what I was supposed to do and how I was supposed to act.

I didn't understand or have any grasp of the fine art of flirtation. I only knew how to go straight to the heart of a thing. I said what I was thinking; I didn't have any tact. And tact is something you really need when you're a teenage girl. Some people are threatened by that kind of directness, but I figured if you're not going to tell people who you are and what you think, you've done them a disservice. They'll have bought a package of goods and they won't be sure what's in it. So I know in high school I must have been kind of goofy, kind of crazy, just willing to do or say anything. There was no Home Demonstration Lady to show me how to grow up as a teenager.

Mama talked to me a lot about how girls must be very, very careful about their reputations. There were some girls in my school, as in all other schools, who suffered from a "bad reputation"—most of them undeservedly. It's such a tough, vicious, mean time of life.

The social life of the Haves revolved around the Fish Pond

Country Club. There was nothing grand about it, but it was the center of that world. My family didn't belong to a country club, but I was usually invited to go play cards by the swimming pool. I never looked like much in a bathing suit, too skinny, so I was never all that comfortable. But I'd go. There'd be the leading socialites—Leta Patton and Barbara Allen and sometimes Kay Coffelt. I'm sure Mama felt it was a big waste of time, but I'd be there at the big umbrella tables learning to play bridge and canasta and samba.

The Fish Pond was where they held all the high school dances, and by the time I was in the eleventh grade I got to go to most of those. There were Valentine's Day dances with construction paper hearts and red crepe paper swirls. All the boys would stand along one wall, and the boys who I wanted to ask me to dance, didn't. Either they didn't dance or they were too shy. I don't think I knew then that boys could be shy.

The band would play "Blue Moon," "Stardust," "Deep Purple." There was one boy named Frank Trapolina who danced with everyone. Frank was a deep dipper, and he was all over the floor. A show-off dancer. Dancing with him was an athletic experience; you'd come away with half the side of your face and head wet from perspiration.

A boy named Morris Warren invited me to dance one day and I came home excited. "Mama," I told my mother, "this darling boy has asked me out!" That was a big mistake. From then on Mama and Daddy wouldn't stop kidding me about that "darling boy." I took a lot of teasing at home about boyfriends. And there was a big thing in high school, if you were going with somebody he would walk you to class, carry your books, and hold your hand. I always felt a little uncomfortable when I had a boy walking me to class, as if everyone was looking at me and making fun.

This is not to tell you that I was some poor pitiful Pearl. I wasn't.

64

*　　*　　*

If I didn't want any attention holding hands in the corridor, I surely didn't mind people listening to me when I talked. My debating had attracted some notice and in eleventh grade I was chosen by the Waco High School counselor, Lulu Strickland, to represent Waco High at Girls State.

Girls State was an annual gathering sponsored by the Women's Auxiliary of the American Legion, in which two representatives from each Texas high school came to Austin for one full week and set up a mock government.

Girls State was run by Frances Goff, who had been in the WACs and was associated with M. D. Anderson Cancer Hospital. She gave her time to the program each summer. Elections were run, bills were passed, and for that week the girls got a taste of what government is really all about. Well, that was pretty thrilling stuff!

The young women at Girls State were supposed to be the cream of the crop. The first thing I did was go around and meet everybody, find out where they were from. I was fascinated. I lived in Central Texas; I didn't know much about the rest of the state. I think I had gone to San Antonio once when I was a kid, and Mama and Daddy had driven me to football games away from home, but this was the first time I had ever met girls from the Rio Grande Valley.

I was hardly even aware that South Texas existed, but they had a wonderful song called "My Valley Home" and I felt a real envy that there were so many girls from these small places and they knew each other's towns. It seemed like a really great kind of community.

Other people might have slipped into a corner and watched the proceedings before diving in, but it was my natural impulse to work the room. If you don't know people, you can't know things. People are my information source, they're the doorway to it all. Unless you are open to them they will never be open to you, you will live in a cocoon. I figured, if you don't meet everybody you won't be able to pick out the ones you choose to be with.

I don't think I was like a Labrador retriever, the kind that jumps up on your shoulders and plants a big wet lick across your face. But let us say that, at the least, I was very outgoing.

At Girls State you could nominate yourself for office. I ran for mayor of my town, then county judge of my county, and then state attorney general.

It was announced that I won! My natural inclination to meet and greet everybody had turned out well. I got to do all the folderol and ceremony of being sworn in. They had a reception for the officeholders at the governor's mansion and Lieutenant Governor Allan Shivers came through and shook hands with each of us. It was a real thrill.

Then I found out I'd lost.

It had been very close, and someone counting the ballots had read a four as a nine. I had actually come in second. I felt terrible for the real winner; I'd shaken hands with the lieutenant governor and gotten all the fun out of it, and she'd actually won the election.

Girls State was fascinating. A lot of elected officials came and spoke with us, such as John Ben Sheppard, who was then attorney general. I was electrified.

Why did I like all this government activity better than I liked anything else? I do not know, but I loved it. I loved it when the men came and explained what they did. It seemed when those men stood up there and talked about their jobs, and talked about serving people, that it must be the finest thing anyone could possibly do.

There wasn't the slightest thought, of course, that I might apply this to my future. Girls simply didn't do that. This was an exercise in learning, it was not an exercise in preparation for a career. That may have been in Frances Goff's mind, but it certainly was not in any of ours.

Even though no one told me, there were certain things that you knew, and the world knew, that women and girls couldn't do. Running the government was one of them. That didn't mean you didn't study or learn about it, it just meant that it didn't apply to you. Any group—blacks, Hispanics, Asians, females—knows that. You know what you're allowed to do and what you're not.

But I didn't consciously think in those terms, I was having such a good time. The following year I went back as a junior counselor, and two more years as a senior counselor.

At the end of the week, two girls were chosen by the counselors and Frances to go to Washington, D.C., to participate in Girls Nation. One of the girls chosen was Mary Garana, who had been elected governor. The other girl was me.

Girls Nation! Even getting there was a treat. We traveled—without a chaperone—by train. I got to sleep in the top bunk and we spent a lot of time staring out the window, watching the states we had only read about roll by. We went down to the dining car to eat dinner, and in those days the service on dining cars was first class. They brought us finger bowls and I had no idea what they were. I don't think I did anything dumb—I didn't drink out of it—but I was truly puzzled.

Girls Nation operated on the same principle as Girls State but on a larger scale. We were taken to the State Department and the Treasury, and met all sorts of dignitaries, including Georgia Neese Clark, Treasurer of the United States, who signed the dollar bills. I thought that was pretty impressive, especially since she was the only female I had seen in any of this business of government.

We went to the White House, into the Rose Garden, and shook hands with President Harry Truman.

Sometime during Girls Nation a group of us delegates were sitting together and had our picture taken. It wasn't any big deal; AP and UPI just had photographers there snapping away. When the photo appeared in the Waco paper it showed me sitting next to a black girl. That's the only thing anybody wanted to know when I came home. Not, How was Girls Nation? or What was it like to meet the president? No. The basic question boiled down to How did this thing happen? and How many black girls were up there? In Waco, young white girls didn't just sit around public places getting their pictures made with black girls. It unfortunately caused a real stir.

3

★

BUT the major story of my high school days was David Richards.

The A&W Root Beer stand was the local summer hot spot. You'd pull up in your car and they would come out and put a tray on the window, and you'd sit and talk and kids would come over. David was sitting at the A&W when I met him. Kay Coffelt introduced us and I thought he was just the nuts.

David came from a good family. His mother had sent him to prep school at Andover for eleventh grade because she wanted him to have a good education, but now he was back. I had been aware of this boy. He was one of those kids who ran around with the Haves, but it didn't make any difference to him. I liked him because he was smart and he had a sense of himself that you could feel from a distance. There was never any doubt in my mind, after meeting David the first time, that he was a very important part of my life

And he was handsome. He had very dark eyes. He was beginning to lose his hair even then, but there was a look about him, a certain presence that said, "I am who I am. Take me on my terms. It's up to you."

I don't know how you know when you connect with someone, but I knew that I connected with David.

We were the same age and the same grade in school, and when classes started again, David asked me out. I was acting in a play at school, *Blithe Spirit,* and David asked me to go out to eat afterwards. We went to the Elite Cafe. It was as good a restaurant as there was in Waco and it stayed open late. Kids would go there and have a cup of coffee and a piece of pie before they went home.

I believe we double-dated. My friend Rusty was going with a good friend of David's named Stanley Chodorow. They went together for a very long time but it was a typically difficult relationship for that day; Stanley was Jewish and Rusty was not.

So there were the four of us at the Elite Cafe and David said in a sort of casual way, "Well, I'm going to order the fried shrimp." I said, "Well, fine. That's fine for me too."

You have to understand, to that point I had probably been into a restaurant half a dozen times in my life. The few times my father and mother and I went out to eat we went to Charlie Lugo's Cafe and my Daddy would order a dozen tamales with chili poured all over them. We would all have tamales, which was a very cheap thing to eat. The only other times would have been at lunch in high school, when we would leave the campus and sit at a counter. You wouldn't be caught dead carrying your lunch in high school.

But it was a *big* deal to go to a restaurant and order a platter of fried shrimp. I think I knew enough not to eat the tails, but I'm not entirely sure.

We had a good time. I talked a lot. I think David found me entertaining.

It turns out that David's mother had seen my picture in the newspaper, the one from Girls Nation next to the black girl, and had said to David, "Why don't you take out a girl like this?"

70

He'd probably bridled at her, but months later, here we were.

My Mama approved of David. I think the fact that he came from a good family was really important to her. He was kind and courteous and he didn't have mud on his shoes. J. B. Little always tracked mud on Mama's carpet.

We went to everything together, parties, the dances at the Fish Pond, and he would walk me to class. I didn't care if anybody looked or talked. It was perfectly natural to be with David.

David was the most interesting boy I had ever met. He was very well read, he was the first person I'd met who had been to a really good school, and he had a value system. He knew what mattered and what didn't. He was impatient with social status, he was loyal, he had a great sense of humor, and he was always game, he loved to do things.

I don't know what it was that David liked in me, but we had a really good time.

David was never preoccupied with clothes. It wasn't that he didn't look nice—he did—it was that he didn't care about it. There was an event in high school called Senior Day, in which everyone dressed in costume. David—all six feet two of him—put on a grass hula skirt with a woman's bathing suit top and a black wig, while I dressed in a sailor's suit my Daddy had got for me in the Navy. I was a sailor home from the wars, and I had brought home a souvenir, which was David. I don't know how I convinced him to wear that stuff, but costumes got to be a continuing thing with us.

The major form of entertainment for us Waco teenagers was the movies. Those were the years of Debbie Reynolds, Mickey Rooney, and the Betty Grable/Dan Dailey She-makes-it-on-Broadway-but-he-doesn't kind of movies. David and I saw a lot of them.

I was a senior in high school when I drank my first beer.

71

There was a roadhouse outside of Waco where a guy named Buddy Woody played the piano and you could buy beer under age. I don't know how much the law was enforced in those days, but it was unquestionably illegal for us to be in there drinking.

The first time I drank too much was on Senior Night. Every year there was a big dance at the Fish Pond and the seniors stayed up all night, sat out in the cars or in the bushes and drank beer, and then in the morning someone gave a big breakfast. I don't know whether I could be classified as drunk or just in a kind of ozone, but I was definitely blazing new ground for myself.

I never drank a lot, but I liked it. I liked the effect of it. Alcohol is a sedative; you don't have to worry, you don't have to feel pain or fear or much of anything. When you're a kid and you drink beer, it doesn't take a whole tankful to get you where you're going.

This was the beginning of lots of beer drinking. David and I were at the roadhouse just about every weekend.

We were spending all our time together and I was learning a million things at once. It was so stimulating to be around someone who knew all the things that I didn't know. Every Sunday afternoon we went to his house for supper, and the talk over the table was like nothing I'd ever heard.

David's mother's name is Eleanor, but my children and I call her Mom El. She came from a well-off Iowa family that owned banks that had gone broke in the Depression, and her family had also owned a major seed company in Iowa. She had graduated from Grinnell College and done graduate work at Radcliffe, and when she came to Texas she was a founder of the Waco League of Women Voters. She was truly an activist intellectual, not some ivory-tower person but a bright and talented woman.

David's father, Dick, had been a football coach at Clemson. At the last game he coached he'd gotten so worked up they had to pack him in ice. That's when Mom El called a halt to his coaching career. Papa Dick was also an engineer, and he had come to Texas on a highway construction job when the Depression hit. The company he was working for went broke and he found himself stranded in Waco.

Somehow Papa Dick began working for a small store, then worked a deal to own it, and built that store into Richards Equipment Company. By the time I met David, Richards Equipment was a thriving business selling machinery and parts in highway construction.

Papa Dick loved to play golf, and he built the family a big, beautiful two-story house near the golf course. It was filled with leaded glass windows, wonderful old doors, a big brass fireplace hood and other antiques they had purchased.

Mom El didn't care much about cooking—she had too many other things to do—so Sunday afternoons Papa Dick would grill steaks or hamburgers and whip up a batch of his famous succotash, and the family would sit around the table and talk.

These were people with political ideas. They took magazines like *The New Yorker*, the *New Republic*, and *Atlantic Monthly;* they had traveled; they talked about what was going on in the state, what was going on in the country. There was an active curiosity about the world.

I had never been around such an atmosphere before. My parents had strong feelings, but whatever politics they talked was what my Daddy heard at work. The Richardses and their friends talked about ideas. It was exciting. This was a world I had heard about but had never been anywhere near.

I felt that I was not equipped, that I could not begin to keep up in this intellectual atmosphere. I'm sure I talked, and I'm sure I talked about things I knew nothing about. But if I did, the family was tolerant of me.

A lot of the time, partly out of anxiety, I would retreat and do the dishes. Doing the dishes is a refuge, it's a place to go when you want to check out; you have an excuse for not being called upon to participate. So I listened and I absorbed everything I could of this very new, very different kind of conversation.

David had it all. Our high school English teacher, Miss Crow, said that David had the best vocabulary in her class, so all of us would tease him and whine, "David Richards has the best vocabulary in Miss Crow's English class." He would use a big word and we'd say, "There he goes."

But David never made fun of people. Mocking everyone around you is a common thread in most teenagers, but David never indulged. He was the only boy I knew who was never cruel.

When David was a child his father and mother read him *Robin Hood* repeatedly. He never tired of the story and they never tired of reading it to him. Robin Hood, Little John, Friar Tuck, Maid Marian, Alan-a-Dale—the characters became personal friends of David's. Intimates. He lived in that world. And each time they'd read it, when they would come to the part where Robin Hood dies, David and his father would cry together.

Robin Hood undoubtedly shaped David's thinking from an early age. He knew, just the way he knew his ABCs, that people without strength had the right and needed the voice to protect their interests. David knew who he was. We would talk about it all the time, it was a recurring theme: "Would Robin Hood have done this?"

David and I dated all senior year. It was a good year for me, I had the boy I loved and I had my debating. My debate partner was a girl name Joanne Sheehy. She was very bright, and, knowing me, I used to tell myself that we won only because she was so smart. Together we won the state debate championships in the Double-A category.

And, oh, we were a precious pair. High school debaters assume an air that is so silly. We wore red skirts with white blouses and navy blue jackets, and each of us had a fake carnation pinned on the lapel. We were pretty good debaters but we looked like the Bobbsey Twins.

We won a tournament at Southern Methodist University and I had my pick of several college debating scholarships. I was not that good a student. I was still making good grades in the things I liked and not so good grades in the things I didn't. But I could have gone to SMU on a partial scholarship, and it was not very expensive to go to the University of Texas, where I also got some kind of a partial scholarship.

I received an offer to go to a girls' school in Lindenwood, Missouri, and if I'd had my druthers I would have taken it. I feel quite certain my life would have been very different if I had gone there. Lots of girls from my class were going away to school and it seemed like such a thrilling, freeing thing to do.

But what it boiled down to was that my parents did not want me to leave home—they simply were not going to let me leave. Baylor was over on the south side of Waco, and the scholarship I received from Baylor paid the tuition. I could live at home.

David and I graduated from high school in 1950. His mother didn't feel he had received a sufficiently good education at Waco High and was sending him back to Andover for a post-graduate year, which didn't sit well with David or me. I also believe there must have been an ingredient in his mother's plans which served to separate us; we were very much in love and we were just children.

So David went East and I went to Baylor.

David came home at Christmas and refused to go back to Andover. Refused. As a compromise, his parents said he could come back and go to the University of Texas in Austin. That worked for a while. He went to UT and would drive home on weekends.

The second semester of my freshman year at Baylor my parents allowed me to move into the dormitory. What a treat! Except for Girls State and Girls Nation and the occasional sleep-over at a friend's house, I had never spent any time out of their home. I got to like it right away.

I pledged a sorority: Delta Alpha Phi. As pledges we had to wear uniforms and carry around a little blue bucket with DAP painted on it, and when any member approached you, you had to turn the bucket over, sit down on it and recite a poem.

But I got a real shock when it came time for the next class to pledge and we had our first rush season session. After meeting the crowd of newcomers who wanted to become DAPs, we all gathered to talk about which girls we would like to have join.

I was stunned by what went on in that room. Some of the pledges had been in the same high school class as some of our members, and our girls started slamming them. It got pretty fundamental: "She slept around in high school."

There was nothing illegitimate about not liking a girl, but that's not where it ended. Judgments were being made on the girls' backgrounds. "Her father's a cop, she's not our type." And if a sorority sister didn't have the guts to come right out and say she didn't like a pledge because the girl didn't have enough status, or enough style, or enough money, she would get around it by saying, "Well, she's just not DAP material."

I don't know what I thought took place in selecting sorority members, but I surely hadn't anticipated this meanness. There was no reason I should have felt any differently about the process than anyone else—I was no firebrand, had no background in any kind of cause. Somehow I just felt that it was wrong to be a part of something where people were excluded for reasons that were not of their own making. It was wrong, and

I decided then and there that I wasn't going to ever do that again. I liked the girls but I left sorority life.

The head of the Baylor Speech Department, and coach of the debating team, was a man named Glenn Capp. We called him "Prof." Prof was a gentle man with a knack of knowing just what to say, whether you won or lost. He was the first person in any kind of authority who made me feel important.

Prof Capp's long suit was logic, the progression one must make from a number of extraneous factual pieces to draw an overall conclusion. He was a good coach, and we held him in the highest regard, not because he was long on technique but because he insisted on substance.

I was never much of an activist. I just kind of took things as they came, but one time I surprised both Prof Capp and myself. The boys' debating team had been invited to compete in the biggest tournament of the year, an all-male event at Notre Dame. It was a big deal, going that far to that prestigious institution to debate. But no plans had been made for the girls' team to take a trip of such grand importance, and I went to Prof and told him that I thought that was unfair and wrong.

I wasn't surprised that he agreed with me—Prof was always thoughtful and logical—but I was very much surprised that he did something about it. He took us on a trip to a debating tournament in Louisiana. Prof was as good as his word.

I was doing well on the debate team and I met a boy named Jim Slatton. I liked Jim a lot. He was on the men's debate team and he was going to become a Baptist minister. Right about then I got religion.

I was saved by Billy Graham when he came through the campus.

Billy Graham was at the beginning of his career then. He was a tremendously attractive, charismatic young man, who would storm around the stage and hold a Bible open with one hand while he preached. He was as glamorous as one-arm driving.

Even though I was "saved," I had a lot of questions about religion. I have always wanted everything to be logical. I don't mind mysteries—in fact, I enjoy a good cosmological magic show—but if it is mystery, I want you to tell me that's what it is. And if it's not, then I want you to explain why it makes sense.

Angels, for instance. Angels have always been the most illogical creatures. When you look at pictures in books or paintings in galleries, very seldom do you see how the wings attach. Angels usually have on long, flowing robes. You stop and think about that: How does the wing get out of the garment? Is there a slit in the back somewhere? How do the angels get them on? The practical problems of robes and wings are enormous. I sewed enough to know.

My friends and I discussed it. One of the possibilities is that angels get their robes at the same time they get their wings, and, on the assumption that angels do not sweat, they probably never change them. They wear them the rest of their angelic lives.

I had a history professor, Dr. Ralph Lynn, who also taught Sunday school, and I talked to him. He agreed that it was not logical, that it really didn't make sense. But, he said, he had faith in a supreme being and a supreme power, and an order and goodness in the world, and if it was necessary in that context for him to believe in angels, then he did. I've never heard a more satisfactory answer to religious improbabilities.

Baylor is a Baptist school, and I went to the Wednesday night religious hour and took all the required religion courses, but I think I was more serious about Jim Slatton than I was about Baptist theology.

Mama didn't like the idea of Jim Slatton at all. He didn't offer the kind of security or life she had hoped for me. Jim was going to be a preacher, and being a preacher's wife is no bed of

78

roses. She couldn't tell me not to see him, but she could move me back home. That was my last semester in a dorm, and when it came to choosing between Jim and David, I chose David.

David's weekend commute from the University of Texas lasted for about a year and a half, and then we just didn't want to be apart anymore. He transferred to Baylor for our junior year. David's mother was disappointed; she was not impressed by Baylor's standards. (When Mom El had come to Waco and wanted to do graduate work, she had applied to take some courses at Baylor. They told her that since Radcliffe didn't accept Baylor's credits, they wouldn't accept Radcliffe's.)

I dropped off the debate team my junior year and lost my scholarship. I didn't want to compete anymore, and I didn't want to take those road trips and be away from David. We were married in May 1953, right after our junior year. I was nineteen.

Most kids we knew got married around that age. Women were allowed to get married at eighteen, but in order to get the license David needed his daddy's signed permission and I teased him about that a whole lot.

Two days before we were married, David's friends threw a stag party at a place down by the river. It was one of those all-night, boys-will-be-boys kind of parties and somehow David managed to scratch his arm on a rusty nail and required a tetanus shot.

The next day, right before the wedding rehearsal, David had a reaction to that shot and blew up like a frog. His face puffed up, he was swollen, he was sick. There was no way he could rehearse. His parents gave a gala rehearsal dinner and he could barely make it down the stairs to put in an appearance.

At the chapel the next day, the service was broadcast over the PA system so "the congregation could hear the vows." Most of what they heard was David whispering, "Which way do I go? Which way do I go?"

We honeymooned in New Orleans. The city was a great

exotic treat to a Waco girl. We combed New Orleans and then moved on to Biloxi, Mississippi. Biloxi is on the Gulf and we were staying at a little motel, and when we went swimming David cut his feet on the coral in the surf.

The next morning he woke up extremely ill. Those were the days when polio was still incurable and very frightening, and we called home and talked to the doctor. Headache, fever, and stiffness were the first signs of the disease, the doctor told us, and David had them all. His neck was terribly stiff. We got in the car and I drove us straight home.

It turned out that David was simply having another reaction to his tetanus shot. But the coral cuts on his feet had become infected and it was fourteen days after we got home before he could get out of bed. There were lots of remarks by my friends that I would take David off on a honeymoon and he couldn't get out of bed for two weeks.

That summer David was working at Richards Equipment and I was working at a dress shop. My new husband weighed 225 pounds and I decided that it was my wifely responsibility to do something about lowering his weight. I found a book on diets and calorie counting—it may have been *The Joy of Cooking,* but I think it was an agricultural extension book, the old Home Demonstration guide—and I set about preparing meals. I had David on a thousand calories a day, which really isn't much for a man who is doing hard physical labor.

We had our own apartment and he would come home for lunch and eat all these green beans and squash that I had cooked for him and whose calories I had so carefully counted, but he didn't seem to be getting anywhere. Well, of course, I found out that he would leave my table each day and go down to the lunch counter and have a big piece of banana cream pie and a Dr Pepper.

Our apartment was lots of fun. The couple next door were

Hoye Jean and Win Biedleman. They came from East Texas—Overton, I believe—and they would get their hometown newspaper, the *Overton Express*, whose logo had a banner underneath it that read, "The Only Newspaper That Gives Two Whoops for Overton, Arp, Leveretts Chapel, and Surrounding Communities." It was full of impassioned editorials and hot mud-slinging. So were Hoye and Win. They were my first exposure to the hot politics of East Texas, and I thought they were great.

I had never been a serious student, but I found out in my senior year that I really did like to learn. I had never known it before. All the spare time I'd had in the past just disappeared; I'd fill it and never know where it had gone. But now I had things I wanted to read, and I didn't have the time to read them. I would go to class and then go straight to the dress shop to earn money.

But that was me: I was having fun and working hard on both fronts, but secretly in the back of my mind I had the feeling that if you're having fun you're not working hard enough. I grew up under the pervasive influence of penance. Mama always told me that if you sewed on Sunday you would have to take the stitches out with your teeth in heaven. So I would temper whatever happiness I was feeling with a good portion of Willis guilt.

4
★

WE graduated in June 1954, and there was a lot of mulling over the question of what David was going to do when he grew up. He had majored in history and there was some talk of his going to business school, maybe Harvard or Wharton, but finally we went to Austin and David enrolled in the University of Texas Law School while I took graduate-level speech and education courses toward my permanent teacher's certificate.

After some practice teaching I got a job teaching social studies to the seventh- and ninth-graders at Fulmore Junior High School. I believe the reason I got that job was that Austin's superintendent of schools, Ernest Cabe, had been the principal of my high school in Waco.

I was barely older than my students. I was twenty, they were about thirteen, though some boys were older. The school system at that time still indulged in "social promotion," which meant that no matter what a student's capabilities, he was promoted. This was to avoid a problem we certainly had had back in Lakeview: some kid can't pass and he gets left back a couple of years and then you have trouble on your hands. If he's some big ol' raw-boned boy he's going to be a real difficulty; too big, too aggressive, more physically and less emotionally mature than the rest of the class.

I found that if you want to be a good teacher there are a thousand situations set up to keep you from it. Our notion of teaching is imparting knowledge. Well, you might get to do that—if you are lucky—twenty percent of the time. The rest of the time you are a referee. You are listening to parents complain, you are listening to students complain. Your administrators are usually guys who couldn't make it as football coaches, or who did make it as football coaches until they started having losing seasons and then got kicked upstairs.

The adjustment from one class to another was enormous. I taught the 7-1's (seventh-grade students with first-grade abilities) to the 9-12's (ninth-graders with twelfth-grade skills). In the 7-1's we would make salt-and-flour maps of Texas. We would mix salt and flour and water, making a gooey paste that we could spread out over the map's outlines. We'd put in the mountains in the Big Bend country and draw little river valleys running down from the Oklahoma border. Of course, with the 7-1's it was a total mess; they would ball up that salt and flour and throw it all over the room.

And I don't think I was equipped to teach the 9-12's. Ninth grade was European history, and while these kids deserved someone who would force their thinking, I was barely one step ahead of them. I would end up giving them rote assignments like memorizing the kings and queens of England, which may have been good enough for the school board but didn't satisfy me.

Teaching was the hardest work I had ever done, and it remains the hardest work I have done to date. The rewards are very subtle, and they are certainly not monetary. Seldom does anyone tell a teacher she is really doing a good job. She's supposed to get her satisfaction by some sort of osmosis, just by knowing it.

In my classes I had many children of migrant farm workers. They would come to school for a while and then it would be time to hit the trail again and they would move on north to wherever they were working. Even when they were in one place they worked hard after school.

I had one little boy who would leave school at three o'clock and go sweep and clean out the barber shop. He wouldn't get home until seven or eight o'clock at night, have dinner, try to do his homework, and go to bed. In class I would look up and he'd be half asleep. You knew the kids who had to work after school; they were simply not as quick, not as alert. There was nothing wrong with their brains, they were bright as could be—they were tired.

David and I were settling in to being married. We were inseparable and, except when we were in class or working, we were always together. The routine was that David would go to school, I would teach school, and every Friday night we would go to the Scholz Beer Garden.

Scholz Garden was a big outdoor drinking establishment with gravel on the ground and big trees shading everything. Rows of folding chairs sat around old wooden tables that had decades of initials carved in them. The place attracted old-time Austinite political activists and a motley assortment of beer drinkers. It had the feel of a real good-time closed fraternity, and we fit right in.

We'd arrive each and every Friday and head straight for the table informally reserved for a group of political folk known as the Horses Association. There would always be some intrigue going on. This was where all the events of any political significance, all the gossip, all the Byzantine political ins and outs were hashed over—and never resolved.

Chief among the Horses Associates were Henry and Mary Holman, Sam Houston Clinton, Marge Hershey, Fletcher Boone. Membership was pretty much a matter of whether there was a seat for you. There were by-laws created when the Horses was originally formed, and I believe Dan Strawn was elected the head of the Horses Association for a ten- or twelve-year term, with Henry Holman as Vice Horse. But there was nothing ever written about how you became a member. It was decided more by attendance than anything else.

In later years the issue became more complex. Wayne Oakes wanted to get in, but Sam Houston Clinton blackballed him. When Sam Houston went to the bathroom they took another vote and he was accepted, so the question remains to this day whether Wayne Oakes is really a Horse.

It was always noisy and raucous at Scholz Garden, with lots of big talk. It was the mid-fifties and the Lyndon Johnson forces were attempting to wrest the power of the Democratic Party from the Allan Shivers forces, the Shivers forces being the conservatives and the Lyndon Johnson forces being the liberals. We were a part of the Lyndon Johnson wing.

I would like to tell you that the conversation that went on around that table was weighty and noteworthy, but by and large it was about who had stolen what convention—all sorts of nefarious planning that never came to fruition. Sam Houston, a veteran of those wars, would be recounting what had happened five or ten years before. This was yarn-spinning; any serious political planning would take place on the side; it would not go on around the table at Scholz's.

David had become interested in the University of Texas Young Democrats and had hooked up with a man named Marion Shafer. Marion Shafer had been a Young Democrat for all forty years of his life. (In those days there was no way you became an Old Democrat, there was no age cut-off.)

You must understand, often in politics being the kingpin

85

of a political group offers you a portion of power that may not be backed up by anything in reality. Even though the Young Democrats had no clout, being the kingpin of the Young Democrats gave you quite a bit. This is the way young people were trained and brought along within the party structure.

The work wasn't fabulously complex. One time Marion Shafer had enlisted David's help in reproducing some flyers to be distributed on campus. The Young Democrats' duplicating machine was a relic that involved putting a piece of paper between two panes of glass and holding it out in the sun to make a print. This would fall to David as his task in the struggle, and he would come home with his head blistered by sunburn for having done his bit for democracy.

Sometime that autumn David was approached to take over the UT Young Democrats, which meant pulling a palace coup against Marion Shafer. We were twenty years old, and the thinking was, "We are the *young* Democrats and as the *young* Democrats we should run the show." So, at the first meeting of the Young Democrats we attended, the coup was performed. David was elected president of the University of Texas Young Democrats.

The problem was, David had never run a meeting before. Here he was president with a full agenda and work to get done. I had taken a course in parliamentary procedure at Baylor, so I became the parliamentarian. I don't remember what we did at that meeting, but I do remember that we carried it off.

Our first precinct convention at Brykerwood School was the confrontation between the Shivers and Johnson forces. Governor Shivers had endorsed Dwight Eisenhower for president. In fact it was predictable; every four years Shivers forces would head Democrats For . . . whoever the Republican nominee happened to be.

The University of Texas has a Homecoming celebration

each fall called Round-up. Round-up was an occasion of great float-building on the part of all the campus clubs and sororities and fraternities, pretty women riding on flatbed trucks, and all the extravagant festivities that go with Homecoming parades. The Young Democrats agreed that we should bring attention to our cause with a Round-up float.

David and I were living in a house on West 31st Street that backed up to Shoal Creek, and the float was to be built in our garage. Being a woman, I was the only one who knew about papier-mâché. But I was also the only one who worked, so the float-building had to go on without me.

Our float was to be an apple. One side was going to look like a good apple, and the other side was going to look rotten. Our message was: "One rotten apple can spoil the Democratic barrel." Meaning, of course, the non-loyalist Democrats.

First we fashioned an apple out of chicken wire. Then we dumped great sacks of flour and some salt into a tub, put the hose to it and created this gooey gunk into which we were going to dip strips of newspaper and build this float. Dave Shapiro was involved, and Ann Klempt and some others. We put this gooey paper stuff on the chicken wire, and of course it would just slide right off. We had a terrible time getting it to stick.

Round-up was rapidly approaching and the rotten apple was not progressing. It reached the point of fish or cut bait.

The good side never made it; we had to make the whole apple rotten. But that was okay, the message would still make sense. Unfortunately, there were these big gaping holes where the papier-mâché wouldn't adhere. We fixed that by putting worms in each of those holes. We made these worms out of chicken wire, but we didn't have time to cover them with papier-mâché, so we put brown paper sacks over them. There were these square-headed worms sticking out of the apple. The whole thing looked more like a blazing Benjamin Franklin stove that someone had beaten with a sledgehammer and stuck in a lot of stovepipes.

This was our first experience at building a float and we were not the best organized in the world; no one had thought to arrange for a truck to haul our creation. We found out quickly that, this being Homecoming, flatbed trucks were in short supply. We sent someone out to try and scare up a truck to put our apple on, and he came back with a truck the bed of which was eighteen feet long. So we've got about a three-and-a-half-foot apple sitting in the middle of an eighteen-foot truck.

We walked the apple to the trailer, which was parked at a filling station, and then hoisted it up. We were standing there looking at this dinky little class project resting forlornly in the bed of this great big old long trailer. Henry Holman and Jean Lee, the grande dame of Austin Democratic politics, were trying hard to be delicate about the disaster.

The next question was, Who will pull this thing? There were no volunteers. We all agreed that it should be pulled by a seedy-looking car—no sense in overshadowing a great political symbol with a shiny auto. Ann Klempt had a Hudson that was the worst-looking vehicle in our crowd, but she was having none of it. Not only was she not going to pull it, she wasn't going to let her car pull it, no matter who was driving.

About that time two eager-looking young fraternity men stopped and identified themselves as being members of the Round-up parade Float Committee. They had driving down Lamar and happened to notice this trailer sitting here and just wondered if this was a float or what.

We got the picture. So, since we couldn't get anybody to pull it anyway, Henry Holman took our rotten apple home and put it in his backyard and his little boys played in it.

But it wasn't all papier-mâché. We took Young Democratic politics very, very seriously. We would hold state conventions and fight for the issues that concerned us just as hard as if we were choosing the president of the United States.

With David in law school I joined the Law Wives. The Law Wives met regularly at the Driskill Hotel to play bridge. We played like crazy for such prizes as corn-on-the-cob holders.

Heman Sweatt, a black man, had sued the University of Texas for admission to the law school, and attended classes in 1950. It opened the door for other black students, and the Law Wives realized that soon there might be a situation in which a black Law Wife might appear on the scene. I was president of the Law Wives David's senior year and I was astounded that there would be a suggestion that the Law Wives might not admit a black woman.

The selection of the next year's president turned on that issue. The woman who won was opposed to allowing a black woman to become a member. She later resigned and the turmoil of the fight reduced the organization to ineffectiveness. I think it ceased to exist shortly thereafter.

Meanwhile, I had been brought up to believe that the greatest fulfillment in a woman's life is to get married and have children, and for some reason I was not getting pregnant. I went to a gynecologist, who told me I had a cyst on an ovary and that it must be removed.

Since I was teaching, I went to the principal and told him, "Mr. Fraley, the doctor tells me that I have a cyst on an ovary and I really need to have the surgery done during the Christmas holiday, so I might be a little late in getting back from Christmas break." He said, "Ann, take my advice and get that thing out, it's just like sleeping with a snake."

I had been led to believe there was nothing to worry about, but Mr. Fraley didn't let it rest. "Of course," he went on, "it's a shame that you're a blonde. You know, blondes have a lot more female troubles than brunettes. I've had those things taken out of my wife that were as big as grapefruits."

Mr. Fraley, for all his comforting words, didn't know what he was talking about. I had the operation.

David had gotten his draft notice and we were both worried that he would be drafted and sent to Korea. On the day he was to go in for his physical, I got the telephone call that confirmed I was pregnant.

David graduated from law school that spring and got a job offer from the Dallas law firm of Mullinax, Wells, Morris & Mauzy. We knew Oscar Mauzy from the Young Democrats. Mullinax, Wells represented organized labor and was recognized as the premier labor law firm in the state of Texas. There weren't more than about three firms in Texas who represented organized labor, probably because there wasn't that much organized labor to represent. Plus, few law firms wanted to do the work. David liked their energy and progressive thinking.

I had given up my teaching job and it was determined by my mother-in-law and my mother that I could not possibly go to Dallas among strangers and have this baby. I was so stupid that I didn't know I could argue. David went to Dallas and lived in Oscar Mauzy's apartment, and I went to Waco and moved in with my mother.

I had been running my own household for more than three years now, I was independent, and it was no picnic living in my parents' house. I wanted to know what was going on with David, how our new life was progressing. Instead, he was starting a new career and I was in my old room.

My mother scared up a tiny newborn rabbit in the yard and brought it to me. I nursed that little rabbit like it was a baby. Then the dog killed it and I had my first child the next day, July 15, 1957.

It was a girl, and I had planned for a long time to name my first girl Cecile. Cecile was the name of my first doll; the Dionne quintuplets were the rage of my childhood and one of them had been named Cecile; I had a college professor named Cecil May Burke; my father's name is Cecil.

David's father's name was Leon, and those people who didn't call him Dick called him Lynn. And I loved my former professor Ralph Lynn, so I named my baby Lynn Cecile. My mother asked, "What are you going to call her? You can't call her 'Seal' because then I'll think of something all slick and wet."

But mother thought the baby was cute, because she was. Cecile was a beautiful baby.

I stayed with my parents for six more weeks and finally, finally moved up to Dallas.

Thank God little babies are pretty strong and resourceful and can usually survive no matter who they have landed with; I had no more idea of how to take care of a baby than the man in the moon.

David was sort of mystified by the whole deal. We had never discussed having children. It was a different era. You didn't think, "Do I want to do this?" or "Is it time?" or "Are we mature enough?" None of these questions ever arose. We were typical of most Fifties couples: we got married; we had babies.

In Dallas we rented a dark little house on Taos Road made out of the ugliest yellow rock; it looked like petrified stone. The back porch was notable because it was cool and damp and attracted the world's largest congregation of slugs. We had two bedrooms, a little living room, a dining room, and a long kitchen.

I sewed a lot and made clothes for the baby and me. I spent one day a week, from morning to night, ironing. I ironed all of David's shirts, because if you took them to the laundry they would tear them up. I cleaned, I cooked, I did what you do.

I cared for Cecile as best I knew how. I would give her a bath every morning, feed her, play with her. In the afternoons I would put her in an infant seat and prop her in the baby buggy and put her in front of "American Bandstand." I'd sit there with my foot hooked in that baby buggy and rock her back and forth, back and forth.

Cecile cried a lot. All first babies cry more than other babies because you have more time to give them attention, so the crying gets results. We were convinced that she had colic. The only time that she really slept was when she was driving in a car, so on weekends David and I would load her in the car and just drive around so she would sleep.

The activities of the Young Democrats took us back to Austin a fair amount. We would drive down there for meetings and weekends, and to visit friends, and every Friday night we would rejoin our political buddies at Scholz Garden.

In Dallas I didn't know many people and there weren't many social occasions. I had one friend named Sydney Ann Bennett who would come over and we would talk. If we felt really adventurous we would go to Luby's Cafeteria at lunch-time and take Cecile with us.

You can't go out looking for friends; they always seem to appear by good fortune. It took a while, but finally, through a woman whose mother knew David's mother, we were intro-duced to people who turned out to be real soul mates: Sam and Virginia Whitten, and Billie and Andrew Holley. We shared our babies, shared our dinners, shared our politics.

David and I would cart our baby buggy to their houses and put Cecile to sleep in some back room, or they would come to ours, and we would sit and drink beer with whoever happened to be in town, or just among ourselves, and we would argue the political arguments of our time. Reverdy and Barbara Glidden, Don and Bunny Bartlett, Virginia and Emerson Titus would pass through and liven the conversation with news from outside Texas.

This was the beginning of integration in Texas. The Supreme Court, in *Brown* vs. *Board of Education,* had ordered the schools integrated in 1954, but "all deliberate speed" was being deliberately slowed to a crawl.

In 1956 Allan Shivers was governor, and he called in the Texas Rangers to "prevent violence," which resulted in stopping the desegregation of a small school district in a town called Mansfield, near Fort Worth. It was not an easy time.

In those days things came to Texas a little later than the rest of the country. The Texas legislature passed a bill outlawing the NAACP in the state. Another made it unlawful to participate in any organization whose aims were desegregation, another demanded public disclosure of all organizations' membership lists, which was intended to intimidate Texans in front of their neighbors. The legislature allowed schools to close rather than follow court orders to integrate.

One of the most impassioned filibusters I have ever heard was conducted by State Senator Henry Gonzalez against measures of this sort. He delivered the notion that no matter what the Texas legislature said or did, these bills if made into law would be unconstitutional. Henry stopped the wholesale passage of these bills into law, but unfortunately, of the thirteen bills proposed, three or four were enacted. Henry was ultimately proved right, though; the Texas Supreme Court subsequently ruled all of them unconstitutional.

Henry Gonzalez later became a congressman from San Antonio.

Unless you have lived under it, the actual feeling of segregation is hard to grasp. You can understand it in a textbook kind of way, but to have lived it is different. It's a rough hand at your throat.

For instance, in Texas, black people were allowed to buy

goods in department stores but they were not allowed to try them on; black women could buy hats but they couldn't put them on their heads. When we held meetings in the Dallas County Court House there were water fountains with signs that said "White" and "Colored" over them, and bathrooms were segregated. If you were black and you were traveling, you'd better pack a lunch, because you couldn't stop in a restaurant and order food. There were no hotels or motels in which you could stay.

When you think what it must have been like, as a child, to be taught not to go certain places, not to look anyone directly in the eye, to keep your head down because if you didn't you might get in trouble—what a terrible life to lead. It was such a self-fulfilling prophecy, the notion that blacks could not do certain work. Well, of course they couldn't; they were never allowed an education that would have taught them to do the work! The schools that blacks attended were not funded as well as the whites', didn't have comparable equipment, teachers, or curriculum. It was an endless cycle, with no break in sight.

Bright young black people who by some miracle had an opportunity to go to school elsewhere never returned home. Why would they? Even if they felt an obligation to return to their communities and make things better they'd find a real fight on their hands and hardly any hope for their children.

The stupidity and self-defeating prevalence of racial prejudice in this country was and is astounding to me. It doesn't allow the economy to flourish. Yes, it guarantees the continuing presence of an uneducated class of people who must work for very little money, but they can't perform the jobs that need to be done.

There was an NAACP in Texas, but it was not very active. A remarkable woman in Dallas name Juanita Craft formed a youth NAACP, trying to politicize black kids, encourage them in school and in life. There were a very few black students who were beginning to enter formerly all-white schools, which was not the easiest atmosphere to be in. I remember sitting in Virginia Whitten's living room, with Cecile on my lap rocking back and forth, listening to Juanita Craft talk about the needs of these young black people and all of us being moved to some action.

But I was by no means a full-time political activist. I was involved in whatever political opportunities I could find, with the constraints of raising a family, which commanded most of my time.

One evening I asked David if he would tend to Cecile and let me go to work in a political campaign. I went over to the NAACP headquarters in East Dallas, in an old house, and stuffed envelopes for Henry Gonzalez's gubernatorial race of 1958. I was invited in by a union organizer we had known from the Young Democrats named Pancho Medrano, and he introduced me to his young sons Richard and Robert, who were about nine years old.

It was my first taste of interracial politics. There were very few opportunities at the time to get to know nonwhite or Hispanic families, and I wanted to know them. I figured you shouldn't talk one game and play another. If you believed that the only way to bring about a peaceful world is to know one another, the only way to get rid of discord is to have familiarity, then you have to do it in your own backyard. Plus, I was thrilled to get out of the house.

David and I rented a house on Kenwell, near Love Field, in a neighborhood that was integrated. Or perhaps I should say integrating; the blacks were moving in and the whites were moving out. At primary election time I put Cecile in her stroller and went door to door, trying to get people to come to the Democratic precinct convention. It didn't work; blacks in the precinct were afraid to go. I assured them that it was legal, that the law-enforcement people would back them up, but they didn't buy it.

There was a real power struggle going on for control of the Democratic Party in Texas. The fight was over loyalty to the party and support of the party's nominees, and also over civil rights, and the disagreements raged from the precinct level to the national party conventions.

In those days "winner take all" was the party rule. If one side in a convention dispute had one less vote than the other, all the delegate strength went to the winning side. The losers went unrepresented. The stakes were so high that a lot of conventions were stolen when delegates were locked out. The only appeal was a "rump" delegation, which would appeal for recognition at the next highest level. If the rump faction convinced the convention that they were the rightful delegates, the original winners were ousted and the rump delegates replaced them.

As a result, the consistent battleground and key to success was the Credentials Committee. The Resolutions Committees saw plenty of action, but the real determination of convention control was in the purview of the Credentials Committee, and the battles were fierce.

The fight had its origins in the old Texas "regular" Democrats, who had fought Franklin D. Roosevelt's nomination and reelection as far back as 1944. They were part of the "Dixiecrat" ticket against Harry Truman in 1948 and opposed Lyndon Johnson in his Senate bid the same year.

In 1952, the forces led by Allan Shivers supported Dwight Eisenhower over Adlai Stevenson in the presidential election, and Shivers was the nominee for governor on both the Democratic and Republican tickets. Ralph Yarborough, an East Texan who was a tenacious campaigner and a magnificent stump speaker, became the leader of the progressive Democratic "loyalist" forces. He ran for governor in 1952 and 1954, and was defeated in the primaries both times by Shivers. In 1956, when Shivers decided to step down, Senator Price Daniel returned from Washington to run for governor and defeated Yarborough in a close race. Yarborough ran for the unexpired Senate term of Daniel and was successful in the special election of 1957.

Lyndon Johnson supporters were successful in defeating the Shivers faction at the 1956 state convention. Frankie Randolph, a Houston woman who had been at the forefront of the loyalist Yarborough group, was elected national committeewoman. But the old animosities lingered and the struggle for control of the party continued, with the progressive Yarborough supporters pitted against the Johnson forces.

David and I supported Ralph Yarborough in each of his races for governor and senator. He and his wife, Opal, had entertained the Young Democrats often in their home when we were at the University of Texas. To this day, Ralph Yarborough receives standing ovations when he enters a room, and he works a crowd as if it were still 1952.

5

★

BY our third year in Dallas, David and I made the first big purchase of our lives, a house on Coogan Drive. David was terrified. I was pregnant with our first son, Dan, and I insisted that we needed a bigger place for the kids to grow up.

It was a nice house and we kept it filled with people. Young Democrats would come from all over the state for meetings and conventions, and we would always throw parties. We'd set up a keg of beer in the backyard and it would cost two dollars to get in, so the keg was paid for. I would make cheese logs, and life just went on.

We fell into a routine. All week long, David would get off from work and go have a couple of beers with the guys and get home around seven or eight o'clock at night. I would cook dinner, iron shirts, look after the children. It started to dawn on me that this is what life was going to be like for a long time.

I was mostly involved with my babies. We did everything by Dr. Spock; if you did not have a Dr. Spock book, you could not raise a child. You looked up everything, but he never told you quite what you needed to know. It was always just short. I never knew. Cecile would be carrying on or Dan would be crying, and my life would be this endless test of, Can I get everything done? I don't think I would have handled it very well if I had not known Virginia Whitten. When I felt myself beginning to get frantic and overwhelmed, I would throw the kids in the car and take the mile drive over to Virginia's.

Virginia had three kids: Lynn, Jeff, and Jill, who was just a little older than Cecile. She was pregnant with her fourth child, Holly. Lynn, the oldest, was a prim and precise little lady; Jeff's nose began to run in December and did not stop until Easter; Jill was a fretful child and would scream and cry and pitch a fit and never go to sleep. I would go over there and it would be bedlam.

I would charge through the door and there in the middle of this storm, with snotty-nosed children crawling, banging, screaming, Virginia would be placidly folding diapers. I had a diaper service, but Virginia washed her own, and she'd be sitting there folding them. "Virginia," I'd babble, "I am just losing my mind." "I know," she'd tell me. "Why don't you sit down and have a cup of coffee."

Somehow, Virginia knew the things that I didn't know. She knew it was passing, that all of this madness didn't last forever. I'd been taught that if there was a glass ashtray on the table, you were supposed to teach your kids not to touch it. (Poor Cecile, we put her through so much discipline.) Well, Virginia knew that it made a lot more sense to pick up the glass ashtray and put it where the kids couldn't get at it.

Simple as that. Kids love to go in kitchens and open all the doors and drawers and take everything out. Why kids do that, I do not know, but they do it. I know people who can't get into their own cabinets because they have rubber-banded them shut. Virginia just moved everything and put spice racks on the insides of the cabinet doors, and filled the racks with empty cans. Her kids went in and out of the cupboard all day, unloading and loading the cans. It didn't hurt anybody, the kids didn't hurt themselves, and they felt like queens and kings.

Virginia was amazing. She is a most gentle, wise, and loving friend. She and her husband Sam came out of East Texas. He was high-spirited, loved to jitterbug, just a dancing fool.

Every weekend we would get together at someone's house, and after dinner David and Sam would argue. They would argue about anything you could name. They would argue with each other, and then if other people were around they would team up and argue with whoever was there.

Sometimes the children would get worried, because Sam and David would be screaming at each other so much. David would shout, "You old fool!" and Sam would yell back, "You silly bastard!" They would get louder as the keg got lower.

One weekend David was exercised on the subject of whether the Junior League does more by delivering its Thanksgiving baskets to the poor than the liberal Democrats do with all their social programs. I don't remember which side he was on; I do know that it was diametrically opposed to the side he had been on the weekend before. I said, "David, I don't understand how you could say that when last weekend you were saying just the opposite."

He didn't look surprised. "Well," he said, "that's how I felt last weekend."

I had never thought of it quite like that. I thought once you believed something you had to believe it forever. David figured that, for the sake of argument, for the mental exercise—for the fun of it—you could take any position you wanted. I had grasped that concept in debating, but this was real life.

Easter was a great time for us. Virginia originated the idea: rather than buy your kid a new Easter basket every year, the thing to do would be to buy a good basket and then hang it out like a Christmas stocking and have the Easter rabbit fill it each year. So we would all get together the night before Easter and have supper and drink beer and listen to David and Sam argue, and put the Easter baskets together.

This was no small deal. We didn't just put a few little things in there. You had to have a toy, and something to wear, and lots of different bright-colored eggs, and maybe a wind-up Easter item. Then you wrapped the whole thing in colored cellophane—a different color for each child—and tied a big bow around it. When it came to our Easter egg hunt, everybody got a lot of everything. I don't think I ever participated in some normal pursuit without turning it into Ringling Bros. Barnum & Bailey.

In 1960 I worked at the Kennedy/Johnson election headquarters in Dallas. I was no insider, but I had someone who would babysit one day a week so I could go down and work the precinct desk. It was menial work like making arrangements for likely Democratic voters to get rides to the polls, or arranging the distribution of the yard signs that dotted our neighborhood, or getting out the bumper stickers.

Dallas was big Nixon territory. Looking at yard signs in middle-class neighborhoods, you'd never have known Kennedy had a chance. The Democrats carried Texas on the magic combination of Lyndon Johnson's considerable clout and John Kennedy's amazingly charismatic character, and Texas was vital in winning the election. It was a thrilling night when Kennedy and Johnson won.

David wanted to go to Washington. He was becoming quite successful at Mullinax, Wells, and had gained great confidence and independence. The number of young people who wanted to be scouts on the New Frontier was considerable, and David landed a job as staff attorney on the Civil Rights Commission. We were very excited as we packed up and moved to Washington.

We rented a house on Capitol Hill in a neighborhood that

was whitening by the minute. Renovators had been buying up row houses in black areas, restoring them, and renting them to white people. The one we lived in had been restored to the extent that they had painted the front of it pink. The neighborhood was very much integrated and in transition when we moved in.

I loved it in Washington. When a foreign dignitary arrived they would hang his country's flag all up and down Pennsylvania Avenue. We had a car, but it wasn't much use; if you took it out and drove somewhere you couldn't find a parking spot when you got back. We walked everywhere.

I took the kids with me to the National Gallery every chance I got. When I was growing up Mama had a picture of the "Blue Boy," and another of a little girl in a white dress called "Innocence," that she'd probably gotten at the dime store. What a thrill to see real Gainsboroughs and Picassos and Degas.

When Alan Shepard went into space they had a big parade and I took the kids down to see him; they didn't want to go, but I did. This was Washington, D.C., and I wanted to take full advantage of it.

I had someone come and babysit once a week, and I would head straight for the Senate. I'd sit there in the gallery and listen to the debate.

I was surprised at the operation's informality. Even though the language was courteous in the extreme, it came as a shock that a senator would be speaking and there wouldn't be more than two or three people in the whole place. I was paying more attention to him than they were.

I was struck by two senators: Hubert Humphrey and Everett Dirksen. Humphrey because of the passion when he spoke; you felt he was speaking from the heart, that he was someone you would like to know. Dirksen, a great jowly leonine man, because he proposed that the marigold be named the national flower. He made a long, impassioned speech about the noble marigold.

On the home front, Capitol Hill was having a problem with rats. All this new construction had disturbed the rodents' home nests, and all the newly restored houses like ours were being overrun. Every evening David and I set rattraps—like mousetraps except scaled for moose—before we went to bed. One hot summer night we heard the trap spring shut.

"I can't face it," David groaned. "I'll deal with it in the morning."

The next morning he put gloves on and went downstairs to the kitchen. A few minutes later he came back. "It got away."

The kitchen was a mess; there had been blood everywhere, but David had very kindly cleaned it up. We thought, okay, we'd try again the next night. I took Cecile to school and came home.

I was sitting at the kitchen table having a cup of coffee with my neighbor Ginger MacKaye when we heard a snuffling sound. We looked over and sprawled on the kitchen windowsill was this sizable wounded rat.

I was a country girl. I'd seen varmints before. We didn't panic. The window was open a little bit and I thought if I could get out into the garden and open the screen, maybe the rat would fall back outside and limp away.

The screen was nailed shut.

I was worried about having Dan in the house, so my neighbor took him to her place and I called David at the office. There was nothing he could do, he said. Call the city; surely they would come get it. He was a little impatient, dealing with civil rights violations while I couldn't handle a little thing like a wounded rat.

I called the city and explained my situation.

"Is the rat dead?" the man from the Sanitation Department asked.

"Well, no," I told him, "the rat is not dead."

"The city only picks up dead animals, they do not pick up half-dead animals."

I called David back. He suggested calling one of our neighbors, Cameron Hoover, who worked at night and was likely home about now. Cameron was a fellow Texan. He had gone to high school with us and married my old debate partner, Joanne Sheehy. I called him.

"Cameron," I said, "I've got this half-dead rat in the kitchen window and I am afraid to fool with it. I don't even know how to approach it."

"Ann, of all people." Cameron was laughing at me. "That you would be afraid of a rat."

"Well, Cameron, it's not that I'm afraid. I just don't know the first thing about how to begin to get at this rat."

"Okay," he smirked, "I'll be down there in a minute."

Cameron walked in with a baseball bat and said in this voice of total disgust, "Okay, where is it?" and walked into the kitchen.

"My God!"

He was backing out as he spoke.

"Get the children out of the house!"

"Cameron, they are out of the house."

"Ann, I can't do anything with an animal of that size." The thing was as big as a possum, and bleeding.

I called an exterminator.

I was sitting in the living room, tapping my feet, with the doors to the kitchen shut, when there appeared at the door this tall, thin, lanky drink of water, the Gary Cooper of the extermination world.

He didn't say much.

"What seems to be the trouble?"

"I've got this rat and it's wounded and it's lying there in the kitchen window."

"All right. I'll go in there and have a look."

We went into the kitchen and he said, "Yeah, well, you've got a problem all right." He reached into the trash can and fished out a number two peach can and an empty box of Kleenex.

I thought, "This is very unscientific."

I don't know what I expected. I probably thought he was going to have a six-foot hypodermic needle filled with poison or something. I also thought, "I need to be out of this room." I went back to the living room and closed the doors.

You've never heard such noise going on. Banging and stomping, squealing and thrashing. I thought, "That fool. He's going to let that thing out in the house."

The doorbell rang. It was the postman delivering a package. He could hear the warfare. "Is there some kind of trouble, ma'am?"

I explained to him that we had set a trap and the rat had escaped and now I had this professional rat catcher back there trying to catch it.

The postman smiled. "I used to run a five-and-dime in New Jersey and we had lots of rats," he said happily. "And the very best rat bait there is, is nutty caramel roll."

We could hear my professional running back and forth, banging, in the kitchen.

"That nutty caramel roll, you get it on the trap and the rat bites it and they can't get their teeth out quick enough, they get stuck in the caramel, and then the hammer flies."

So I'm having this engaging conversation about rat bait with my postman and the rat catcher emerges. He is holding the Kleenex box, which is holding the peach can, from which is dangling this very long rat tail. The rat catcher still isn't saying much.

"I'm very grateful," I offer. "How much do I owe you?"

"Thirty dollars."

He could have said a thousand and I would have written the check.

I'm writing while he and the former-dime-store-owner-turned-postman are engaged in discussing the merits of various baits in rat catching.

They leave together.

I go across the street to retrieve the kids and turn to watch the rat catcher as he walks down the sidewalk. He gets to the corner, leans down, takes the rat, the can, the Kleenex box and all, and drops them through the sewer grate.

But Washington wasn't all Senate speeches and rattraps. David was in government and we knew the Texas crowd. Mary Margaret Wiley, who was Vice President Lyndon Johnson's secretary and assistant for a number of years, was a friend from the old days in Austin, and she invited us and a half-dozen other Texans to a small birthday dinner at her house. We were youngsters—I don't think I was twenty-nine years old at the time—and we were sitting around drinking and telling stories when Vice President Johnson himself arrived.

We were all dumbfounded. Mary Margaret worked with the vice president all day, but the rest of us had no access to him at all. This was a mountain of Texas myth walking amongst us.

Johnson was the last of the truly powerful vice presidents and he was an enormous asset to President Kennedy. You weren't dealing with any rinky-dink senator, you were dealing with the Senate majority leader, one who had been through Congress, who knew where all the nuts were buried. And although he was now working in the executive branch, his command of the ebb and flow of political life in Texas remained awesome. It was clear from his presence alone that this man was out of our league.

You have to understand the way and drift and nuance of

politics. When I first got involved with the Young Democrats, the Johnson wing was the outpost of Texas reform, fighting the power forces led by Allan Shivers. Once Johnson won, he became the power, and the forces of reform were led by Ralph Yarborough. As power swings, there will always be a movement to replace it. We were young, we were reformers, and we were looking at as much established power as any of us had ever seen in one man.

None of us knew quite what to say or how to talk to him. David, to make contact and conversation, mentioned an article he had read recently in the *Texas Observer* that was extremely complimentary toward the vice president. Johnson chose to ignore that article and launched into a tirade.

Another article in the same issue of the *Observer* had had to do with the hard fight against red-baiting in the 1950s. It was written by Maury Maverick, Jr., a former Texas legislator, and it focused mostly on what he, Maury Maverick, had done or withstood during that period. Apparently the article had not mentioned LBJ to his liking, and Johnson had taken it as an affront.

Johnson was a large man with a powerful voice. He spoke with authority and cut a large wake. Standing in Mary Margaret's living room he was like an ocean liner in a small harbor. He was not a man you wanted to have an argument with about anything. He took out after Maury Maverick, Jr.

Johnson began citing chapter and verse of how he, Lyndon Johnson, had been decisively instrumental in censuring Senator Joe McCarthy. It was clear that Johnson felt very strongly about the role he had played, and that Maury Maverick was in a world of trouble for omitting him. He was roaring. For good measure, Johnson went on to denounce Frankie Randolph, a woman of considerable prominence and money, who owned the *Texas Observer*.

The discourse went on for some time, and no one even considered interrupting. Standing with drinks in our hands as Johnson railed against Maury—we knew Maury Maverick, he was a good man—we felt as if we had walked into a blast furnace.

As I remember, that was pretty much the end of the party.

6

★

AT first, David enjoyed his work. Ironically, after his years defending labor unions, he was assigned to investigate discrimination in them. I don't know whether his immediate superiors knew his background, but he was sent to one Southern state to look into why there were no blacks in the plumbers' union. He talked to the man in charge and was told, "Everybody knows blacks can't do plumbing." Except the guy didn't use the word "blacks." At the electricians' union they told him there were no blacks because blacks were afraid of electricity. It would have been funny if it hadn't been so sad.

David liked what he did for a while. But after having been autonomous and very much in charge of his own cases in Dallas, he had a hard time adjusting to the Washington bureaucracy. He would write a report and it would go through three or four other hands, and by the time the final report got written it was hard for him to find even a legend of what had originally been his.

David had been involved in the decision-making process and I never had, but I was an activist and for my part, there was nothing to do. The entire time I was there the only thing asked of me was to bake cookies for the Capitol Hill house tour.

The politics of Washington is the work of Washington. It's not an avocation. We had looked forward to meeting and being involved with the best and the brightest, and we would go to some social events, but after the first six months we began to tire of the eternal speculation about which senator was sleeping with which other woman. We pretty quickly came to the conclusion that when we had moved to Washington we had left the New Frontier. In February 1962, a year after we had arrived, we went back to Dallas.

David went back to work at Mullinax, Wells. We bought a wonderful old house at the corner of Athens and Lovers Lane. And I was pregnant again.

Our third child was a boy. Clark. He was a very serious baby. He didn't laugh or smile a lot, but he was a cuddler. I used to love to rock and sing to my kids, but Dan was a squirmer, he didn't like to be still, he was afraid that he would miss something if he fell asleep. Clark loved to be rocked and held, and I rocked and held him. He was also terrifically resourceful and took care of himself. When he grew older we could put one of those miniature boxes of cereal in bed with him, and he would wake up in the morning and sit there and eat his cereal and not wake anybody.

Once I got back to Dallas I wanted to be involved in everything. We formed the North Dallas Democratic Women, an organization that worked on the grass-roots level to elect loyal Democratic precinct chairmen, convention delegates, and candidates. The issues were generally race and loyalty; there were still elected Democrats who would form committees to support Republican candidates, and we wanted that stopped.

But the basic struggle was what it's always about: power— who was really going to have the stroke that sets policy, passes laws, chooses the national Democratic presidential candidates. It was no small amount of power, and no small amount of infighting. One county commissioner's race was so tight and could have been stolen so easily that the night after the election David and several other men went down to the courthouse and slept with the voting machines.

The North Dallas Democratic Women was basically formed to allow us to have something substantive to do; the regular Democratic Party and its organization was run by men who looked on women as little more than machine parts. It wasn't that I didn't like the men I worked with on campaigns; I did. It was just that we women did all the dumb work, were never allowed to make any decisions, basically didn't use our brains. No woman ever moved up in that organization.

As our network of women grew we decided we needed to have some ongoing system for keeping up with precinct workers and people we could call on to do good work from campaign to campaign. We transformed one of our upstairs bedrooms into something of an office with cards and files everywhere. Ruthe Winegarten, Ann Chud, and I don't know who all trucked in on a regular basis to update those card files and add names. Dan Weiser was a real mentor, and we used the files to find Democratic loyalists who we might convince to run for precinct chairs.

I was president of the North Dallas Democratic Women at one time, played a role in putting together an organization linking all the Democratic clubs in Dallas County, then served as president of that group.

We formed an organization called the Dallas Committee for Peaceful Integration. The whole idea was to show that not everyone in Dallas was fighting the notion that white and black children should go to school together. Ours was certainly a minority view in Texas at the time.

I felt it was simply the right thing to do. If your Christian beliefs, your "Love thy neighbor as thyself," meant anything at

all, then you had to believe that it was only right that all children have the same opportunities. I could understand individual dislike—you're not expected to love everybody—but I could not understand class hatred, and especially that it would extend to children.

The Dallas Committee for Peaceful Integration probably had around forty members. It was the most law-abiding group imaginable. But this was the time of J. Edgar Hoover, and any organization was fair game. One morning the papers were full of an exposé by an undercover FBI agent who had "infiltrated" our committee. Infiltrated, my hind foot. This wasn't some closed group with a secret purpose; we ran open meetings and anybody could join who wanted to join. All of a sudden the state wanted to smash us. We hadn't known we were any big deal.

To raise money to support our North Dallas Democratic Women activities, Carolyn Choate, Ruthe Winegarten, and I had the grand idea that we would stage shows similar to the Gridiron spoofs done by the press. Writing the shows was great fun. Carolyn and I had known each other in Law Wives at the university and she is a talented pianist. Ruthe and I were idea generators and helped Carolyn with the scripting. We called the extravaganza "Political Paranoia."

Casting the first show took a lot of convincing of our members, who had a real reluctance to making fools of themselves in front of their friends. But convince them we did, and "Political Paranoia" was a real hit. In the following years we had fights for the plum parts, and we played to packed houses in whatever high school or church would rent us space.

Joyce Schiff was always the star. She was the most gorgeous and seductive-looking of all of us and she would wear fishnet stockings and a black leotard and walk across the stage like a showgirl between rounds at a prize fight, carrying signs announcing the next act.

Each of the skits lampooned local, state, or national figures. I played Lyndon Johnson in one of them, dressed in a suit, a cowboy hat banded by a glittering crown, and trailing a sweeping red satin train. I sang, "This land is my land, this land is my land, this land is my land, this land is my land. . . ."

One of the most elaborate numbers, in 1968, was "The Wizard of Odds." Several Republicans were vying for the presidential nomination and we dressed them as Oz characters. George Romney was the Scarecrow, Nelson Rockefeller was the Cowardly Lion, and Richard Nixon was the Tin Man. Ronald Reagan was in it too; I think we had him dressed as a clown. And of course Shirley Temple was Dorothy. Their song, to the tune of "If I Only Had a Brain," seems more than a little dated now, but the night of the performance it was a smash!

Romney   *I have had some trouble thinking*
And I know it's not from drinking
But I just cannot explain
Why my left hand's on my right side
And my right hand's on my left side
Well, they must have washed my brain.

Rockefeller   *I have Happy, I'm Go-Lucky*
And I have no inspiration
For the Presidential craft.
I am easy to discourage
And I know I'd find the courage
If I only had a draft.

Nixon   *Here's your slicky, Tricky Dicky*
Coming back to make you sicky

Would you like to buy a car?
Well, I have the same old stuffing
Filled with absolutely nothing
Don't you wish I had a heart?

Reagan   *Oh, I know that I'm a cutie*
Just a little Tootie-Fruitie
But I want to have my day.
I can sing and dance and yo-yo
I'm a Hollywood-a-go-go
And I want to run and play.

Shirley Temple   *On the Good Ship GOP*
It's a groovy place to be
We'll sing and dance
Every single time we get the chance

On the Good Ship GOP
Everyone a star can be
Do a heel-and-toe
Then you can shuffle off to Buffalo.

Our home became like a revolving door at the Waldorf. We had people coming in and out, visiting; at least twice a week there was somebody sleeping overnight in the den. It was constant. And the house was always filled with kids, mine and everybody else's. Any time anybody needed a place to meet, they met at our house. And any time anybody met there that meant they had to have something to eat and something to drink.

But I wasn't complaining. Far from it. I enjoyed being the hostess for all these proceedings, and having our home as a hub of activity brought the outside world in. I had three kids, if it didn't come to me there wasn't any way that I would know about all these goings on. I was happy to be part of politics when I had the opportunity. Certainly it was something that occupied a great deal of David's time and attention, and it was an integral part of our social life.

As a result of our activity we found ourselves on the list of Dallas folk who would entertain foreign dignitaries when they came to town. We wouldn't get heads of state, though; we would get the more unusual guests. I think the State Department had some difficulty in Dallas finding people to entertain black visitors.

Once we were asked to entertain a Nigerian diplomat named Prince Eze Okoli. In an effort to give the prince a good impression of the United States, and to emphasize that blacks and whites saw each other socially, we invited a Dr. and Mrs. Powell, whose son was in preschool with Dan.

I'm sure there was some considerable talk around the house that week about the fact that a prince was coming to dinner. I got out all the best linens and dressed the table suitably. The evening came and the prince walked in.

Prince Eze Okoli was about five feet tall and weighed around two hundred and fifty pounds. He was wearing some kind of flowing robe costume with food stains all over it—it couldn't have been washed in weeks—and a porkpie hat. He was generally an all-around unattractive fellow, accompanied by a member of the State Department.

Cecile was about six years old and during dinner I saw her at the far end of the den, peering around the doorway. It was past her bedtime, and I got up and went into the hallway. She looked at me with big storybook eyes and said, "Mama, is that a prince?!"

It dawned on me that she had undoubtedly been expecting some handsome brute on a white charger. I laughed and told her it was. I thought that it was appropriate that Cecile learn at a very early age that Prince Charming would probably not appear, and if he did he might be five feet tall and fat and wearing dirty robes.

Also around that time the farm workers were really beginning to organize in the valley farms of South Texas. Cesar Chavez had already come to Austin and delivered a speech, and we had gone to hear him and been very much impressed. Now they had scheduled a march from the valley to the state capitol. We decided to drive to Mission, Texas, where the march was to begin.

The night before, the farm workers held a dance in a VFW hall or perhaps it was just some storage building for a Catholic church. It was hot and dusty, but when we walked in the music was wonderful and lively, and people were dancing, ranging around the whole floor to blaring mariachi trumpets.

Cecile was probably ten or twelve years old and she looked over at me with a big smile on her face and said, "You know, Mama, this is my first dance!"

I like that story. Perhaps that's what all first dances should be like, hot fun for important causes. That kind of reality will serve you in a lot better stead in adult life than romantic notions.

Two UFW organizers, Ernie Cortez and Frances Barton, came to Dallas to focus the drive in our area around melons from a company named La Casita. They tried to get through to the grocery stores to convince them not to sell La Casita melons, but of course none of the store managers would see them.

I met these organizers, who were still only teenagers, and their cause seemed very worthwhile to me. So when I was asked to help I stepped in. I would wear my most matronly outfit and go into the store and ask to speak to the manager. When he came out to see me I would introduce him to Ernie and Frances and they would give him the pitch.

We made some headway, but the store owners got smart; they would take the labels off the melons. So it became necessary to go around into the alley and see if there were any La Casita crates back there.

I can truthfully say that the only grocery not to sell La Casita melons in Dallas was the one I patronized in University Park. I went in and told the store owner that this was a matter of some seriousness to me, and a matter of a very serious nature to the people who harvested these crops, and I would appreciate it if we didn't see any more La Casita melons in my A&P. I bought so much food there, feeding the arriving hordes, that I was a valued customer and he didn't want to lose me, so he agreed.

But I don't want to paint my role in these political doings as one of any significance. Most of what I did was make phone calls and stuff envelopes. I wasn't an organizer, I didn't set the agendas or do any of the important planning. I was a peripheral player.

In books like these, and in historical treatises, it's easy to list dates and times—this event took place here; that happened then; he ran; he was elected. But by and large that's not what's going on in people's lives; most of them are just trying to get along, to make their families comfortable and themselves happy. No one talks about that very much, as if those things are not significant enough. I want to emphasize what I was doing. What was really going on from day to day in my life was birthday parties for little kids, Easter egg hunts, Indian Guide meetings, Campfire Girl meetings, Girl Scouts, ironing shirts, cooking large quantities of food not only for a good-sized family but also for parties and meetings. This is what went on at our house all the time. All the time.

I was running a household, catering the local Democratic Party, being everything to everybody. I had a wonderful time, but there were moments when I felt that there was probably something more to life and I just didn't know what it was. I took up bird-watching because it was something I could do at home. I was always painting a room or re-covering a chair, or out in the garage trying to create a playroom for the kids. There just was never a moment that I wasn't doing something for someone.

Dallas in 1962 was an angry town. While we finally had some semblance of integration of the public schools, we didn't have integration of private facilities. Blacks still couldn't eat in public places. We were still living in outright segregation. The Dallas Committee for Peaceful Integration had a real fight on its hands.

A retired general, Edwin Walker, had appeared on the scene and was loudly equating President Kennedy, and anyone who supported him, with communism. It was military tradition, he announced, that the flying of the flag upside down was an indication of distress, and he was given to flying his flag upside down in his front yard. There was a sizable portion of the population that was in agreement with him.

Some Dallasites thought the United Nations was a communist organization. There were newspaper editorials to that effect. Adlai Stevenson, the United States ambassador to the United Nations, was speaking at a United Nations Association–sponsored lecture while a band of men in black shirts, black pants, and black boots goose-stepped up and down on the sidewalk in front of the hall, giving the stiff-armed salute. Inside there were hoots and catcalls, and when Stevenson began to speak he was drowned out by an orchestrated pack of women who jangled their charm bracelets so loudly he was forced off the stage.

Republican Congressman Bruce Alger, who had represented the district, was not what one would call a mainstream Republican; he was considerably to the right of that. One day when Vice President Johnson and Lady Bird Johnson were in Dallas, Representative Alger's sympathizers put on their best finery and picketed them at the Adolphus Hotel. When the vice president and Mrs. Johnson emerged from their car, this group of Dallas' leading ladies, in the trappings of wealth and civility, battered them with picket signs and spit on them.

It seemed I was fighting an endless and very personal battle. I would read the morning newspaper and become either very depressed or furious. There was a strong voice in Dallas who felt that if you didn't agree with them you were either crazy or a communist.

"Goldwater for President" signs had already begun appearing on lawns and car bumpers around Dallas. Lyndon Johnson called Stanley Marcus, the founder of Neiman-Marcus and an active Democratic fund-raiser, to say that President Kennedy was coming to the city, and in order to host the luncheons and dinners that go along with such a visit, it would be necessary to raise some money. Lord knows, that is a constant in politics.

Marcus told him, "Lyndon, don't come." He was very insistent about it. "You know what it was like when you and Lady Bird were here," he said, "you were spit on and hit with picket signs. Don't bring Kennedy to Dallas."

I don't think anyone thought that anything seriously untoward was going to happen to the president, but there was this general unease, the sense that it was not a healthy atmosphere for the president and it would just be better for him to go somewhere else.

119

President Kennedy was scheduled to attend several functions while he was in town and the competition for tickets was fierce. John Connally was governor, Ralph Yarborough was senator, and everyone was hoarding. I had a hard time, but finally the night before Kennedy was to come I managed to scout up two passes to the luncheon in his honor.

It was to be held at the Dallas Apparel Mart, a big open multistory indoor atrium with an interior courtyard and balconies around each level. When we got there the main floor was filled with tables for the well-connected, and your place in the political pecking order was pretty well established by the distance of your seat from the dais. I was up on the third level. I looked above me and there were birds, lots of parakeets flying around loose up in the building's girders. Our food had been served, and I sat there thinking, "We better watch out for these birds."

There was an announcement that the president had been delayed. Someone behind me had a radio and was following the progress of the motorcade, and word filtered through that President Kennedy had been hurt. I looked down onto the main floor and saw a clot of press people start to run toward the back of the room. Only then did it dawn on me that something was seriously wrong.

Dallas' mayor, Erick Jonsson, who was hosting the luncheon, came to the podium. He told us that the president had been shot. The atrium was silent, as if everyone had inhaled at once and was holding it.

I remember being terribly afraid. The only thing I could think was that I had to get home.

The escalator down was overwhelmed. More people were crowding on than could get off at the other end, and panic set in. People started raising their voices, there was a crush at your back and nowhere to go. The fear in the building was physical.

On the radio in the car on the way home we heard that the president was dead.

They closed the schools and sent all the children home. The kids in Cecile's class applauded when they heard that Kennedy had been shot.

Very shortly after, David came home. It was everybody's instinct to go home, to find a safe place. If it could happen to the president, it could happen to you. The rest of the weekend was like a nightmare.

We were, like everyone else, glued to the television in a state of shock. Except here we were in Dallas, and all of these horrifying incidents that you were used to seeing in quick news clips from other people's streets were happening in our own backyard. Officer Tippett confronted Lee Harvey Oswald in a Dallas movie theater and got shot. Oswald was arrested by Dallas police. We knew these locations, we had driven past that theater.

Lots of times, upheavals and catastrophes seemed "played out" on stages that are very far away. You see it on television, as if an earthquake or an assassination were some sort of international theatrical experience. Not this time. These were national upheavals on a personal level, and we in Dallas were taking it personally.

David finally had enough. He said, "We've got to get out of this. We can't continue to sit here in front of this television." We called the Whittens and the Holleys, grabbed the kids, and headed to the country for a picnic.

When we got back to town we found that Jack Ruby had shot Oswald.

The assassination was so bizarre, so completely crazy, impossible, insane, that it provoked a spasm of self-examination among a great many of the powerful and responsible people of Dallas. When you mentioned the city, from that moment on the first image that came to mind was that Dallas was where President Kennedy had been shot. That alarmed the people who ran Dallas. "We cannot allow our town to have this image," they thought. "We cannot allow this atmosphere to continue."

The city felt personally responsible. Local newspaper and magazine stories always asked the question, Could this have happened anywhere else? It was a constant. At first the answer was, "If you have a deranged person, that madman can act anywhere." Memphis, Los Angeles, anywhere. But in the aftermath, Dallas began to question whether or not this was the kind of community they wanted it to be.

There was nothing specific you could point to as evidence, but the people of Dallas—not the politicians with a career stake in the city's image, but the people who lived there and actually made up the city—began to say, "Hey, we want to be liked. We want to be known as a community where people want to live, we don't want to be known as some fringe-element lunatic asylum."

7

★

THERE were a lot of pregnant women at our 1963 Easter egg hunt. Three couples were having children, adding to our sizable circle of friends and relations. David had been feeling poorly for several days, but he hung in there and played the good host as kids ate cookies and went scrambling for hidden eggs. That night he had a high fever and the next day we took him to the doctor. We were worried that he'd had a reoccurrence of mononucleosis.

It turned out he had German measles, and had exposed all of these pregnant women to it in the process. We called them and told them they needed to get gamma globulin shots for protection. They were not happy to hear from us. Later that evening David said, "You don't suppose you could be pregnant, do you?" "No," I said, "no way, not possible." Then I started counting and, sure enough, I was. I went and got the shots too. Our second daughter, Ellen, was born fine and healthy in November.

I had had high blood pressure and ended up delivering Ellen by cesarean section. When I came home from the hospital I was weak and tired and not at all well.

A few days later I started hemorrhaging. There was so

much blood and I couldn't stop it. I was truly frightened. I thought I was going to die.

David wrapped me in a big old pink comforter, laid me down in the backseat of the car, and rushed me to the emergency room. I lay there bleeding and shivering, and I remember thinking that I was not afraid to die. I didn't want to die, but I consciously thought how fortunate I was to have had my children, to have David, to have had so many friends. What more could I ask from life?

I spent New Year's in the hospital, with David and friends taking care of my baby. The doctors gave me shots and fed me through IVs and nursed me back to life.

I had always been afraid of flying, but after that I never was. Basically, I think fear of flying is fear of dying, and I had faced that.

I have never worried about being sick and I have a very high threshold of pain, I can stand a lot. But this began a saga of illnesses.

Virginia Whitten and I took the children on a picnic one day that spring and had a car packed full of kids. We were such a close-knit group that it always seemed like we had eight kids total, instead of dividing them up her four and mine. It made life more exciting, since every little event became an outing. I was driving the bunch of us home that afternoon when I blacked out. Thank God Virginia was in the car; she grabbed the wheel, eased on the brake and pulled us over. I had totally blacked out. My eyes closed, my head rolled.

A couple of months later my mother was in Dallas visiting us and I had another attack. This one was pretty severe. I went to the hospital and the doctors couldn't figure out what was wrong with me.

When I had the third one, my doctor asked me to tell him everything that happened when these things came over me, down to the last detail. It finally came to him. "My God," he said, "you're having grand mal seizures!"

So, I was epileptic. They put me on a drug called Dilantin, which is supposed to reduce the number of messages to the brain and, as a result, eliminate the seizures. I never had a major seizure again. Oh, every once in a while I would have what is called a *petite absence,* which can be brought on by the flashing black-and-white effect you get walking by a picket fence and sends you out for a moment or two. but I never had another major attack. I started taking the drug when I was in my thirties and continued it for fifteen years. I'm done with it now.

But my troubles weren't over. David and I were installing new doors on our house, staining them with a terrible-smelling finish, when I got a headache that wouldn't quit. It was horrific, as if someone were digging at my eyes with an ice pick—from the inside. And it would not go away. I have a high tolerance for pain, but it reached the point where it was so intense that I didn't think I could stand it. We drove straight to the doctor and he told me I had encephalitis.

I wasn't the first. There was an encephalitis epidemic in Dallas and there were already government people out in the field to handle it. So there I was sitting in my hospital bed in a fancy black nightgown that David had bought for me, David and I were playing cards, and this government man from the health department comes by to try and nail down the source of my disease. He was very respectful, making his rounds, and he asked me whether my house was on stilts and if we kept chickens under it.

I guess the government health department had developed a standard set of encephalitis epidemic questions, and stilts and chickens were both on it, but the idea of having a house on stilts with chickens under it in University Park in Dallas struck me as pretty ridiculous, and I told him so.

*   *   *

Once I finally got out from under my siege of diseases I was raring to go. Tony and Claire Korioth and a group of people we knew were going to canoe down Boquillas Canyon on the Rio Grande, and asked if we wanted to come. I had never been in a canoe in my life, and if David had it was twenty years earlier, when he went to summer camp. But we were game.

We're talking about getting into a major river with some pretty tough rapids, but Tony and Claire were good friends. Tony had been in law school with David and had married Claire, whose daddy was a Dallas judge; they wouldn't steer us wrong.

Also on the trip were, among others, Neil Caldwell, who had been in the Texas legislature and is now a judge in Angleton; Joe Christie, who had been in the Texas Senate and is now in the gas business; Warren Burnett, a very colorful trial lawyer from Odessa; Malcom McGregor, a charming El Pasoan who had been in the Texas legislature; Willie Morris, a writer who had been editor of the *Daily Texan* at UT when he was a student and went on to be editor of *Harper's*; Bill Kugle, a former legislator who now practices law over in Athens; Mr. Democrat Henry Holman, the Vice Horse down at Scholz Garden; and Anders Saustrup, who was something of an expert on native Texas plants. So it was a big, big flotilla of politicos.

David was too vain to wear his glasses to canoe down the Rio Grande. I don't know whether there was any connection, but my father-in-law had given me a wrist strap that, when you punched it, would release water wings on each wrist. I wasn't that good a swimmer.

Amid lots of threats and promises, our armada put into the river. We were perhaps ten minutes into our adventure when I said to David, "Which side of that rock do you want to go on?" David said, "What rock?"

We hit it sideways. The rapid just dumped us right out,

filled the canoe with water and wrapped it clear around the rock. I was still fiddling with this damn thing on my wrist trying to sprout my water wings when David and some others drug me out of the river.

When you get into river canyons, the only way out is down. You don't just get up on the bank and walk out. I don't know if I would have left if I could have, but there was nothing to do but get back into the boats and go. David got in with Joe Christie, who had been canoeing by himself, and I got in the center of Tony and Claire's. Our boat became known as Tony and his Oars. Much laughing and snickering about that.

David's and my canoe was a total loss; we just left it there. Stories abounded when people came upon it, and from what I hear it is now the stuff of legend. We've heard all sorts of tales. One had it that they were shooting a movie down there and it had been a prop. Another said a guy was canoeing and saw it, overturned, broke his glasses, broke his nose, and had to continue down another three days on that river with fractured eyesight and a busted nose.

But we loved being on that river. Most of our bedding and such had been packed in Army surplus rubber containers and was saved, and we went on and ran some pretty rough rapids.

There's something liberating about canoeing a river. The sunlight on those canyon walls gives them a honey-pink glow in the mornings, and as the day goes on it burns into a brighter orangy red. Then as the day fades they get dark and at night they're totally black. It's a wonderful light show.

We took many river trips after the first one. Once, down Mariscal Canyon, I was lying on a grassy bank looking up at the slit between the top of two canyon walls, and a peregrine falcon just darted and sailed back and forth across that little ribbon of light. If you ever feel religious or close to God, it's at a time like that.

David decided that he ought to be able to collect all the

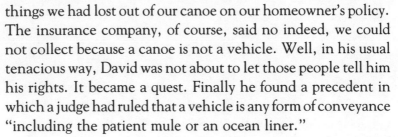

things we had lost out of our canoe on our homeowner's policy. The insurance company, of course, said no indeed, we could not collect because a canoe is not a vehicle. Well, in his usual tenacious way, David was not about to let those people tell him his rights. It became a quest. Finally he found a precedent in which a judge had ruled that a vehicle is any form of conveyance "including the patient mule or an ocean liner."

David collected under that homeowner policy. And quickly sent letters to everyone who had taken that trip to let them know that from now on if they lost anything, on the back of "the patient mule," they could collect on it.

My specialty was camp cooking. All the provisions people will sell you lots and lots of this dried stuff and tell you that the astronauts loved it, but if you plan the trip right you can take along fresh food.

You can start the first night with a vegetable or beef stew; then you can add fresh carrots and potatoes and celery. If you make enough and the weather's not too hot, you can pack the leftovers up in plastic containers and have them the next night. You can do great things with loaves of brioche or really good French bread hollowed out and stuffed with scrambled eggs and sausage.

So, again, I was never really satisfied with just going camping or just going canoeing; it had to be a gourmet experience.

One Easter week David decided he wanted to take a canoe trip down the Buffalo River in Arkansas. He figured I should stay home and mind the kids, it being Easter week with festivities coming up. He asked me if I minded putting together "just the necessities, just the basics" for him to take.

So Phyllis Kultgen and I went to the grocery store and shopped for "just the basics." We had a real good time. Then I set about putting together these packets of food for the river trip: Breakfast, Day 1; Lunch, Day 1; Supper, Day 1; Breakfast, Day 2; and so on.

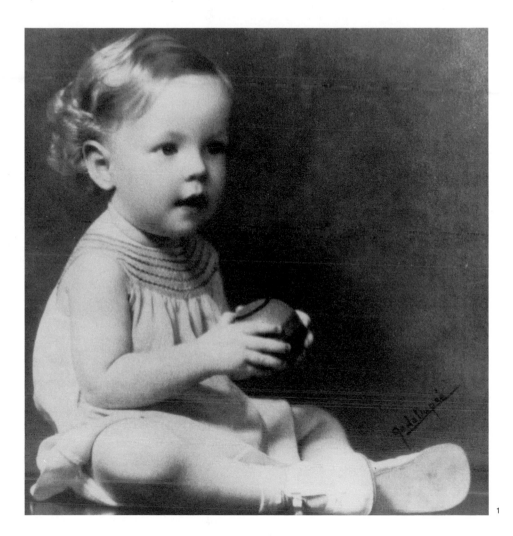

1

I was born in a little country house down a dirt road in
Lakeview, Texas. I don't know why in the world it would be
called Lakeview; there was no lake to view.

2

3

Top: My Daddy and Mama, Cecil and Iona Willis, never wanted me to work as hard as they did. But that was all I ever saw them do, and the message I got was that the only thing of any real value in life is hard work. *Bottom:* My high school debate partner was a girl named Joanne Sheehy, and together we won the state debate championships. We were pretty good debaters, but we looked like the Bobbsey twins.

Top: First and foremost, I was a Mom. I learned more about management from running a household than I have from any other single occupation. Here I am with (*from left*) Clark, Cecile, Ellen, Dan, and David. *Bottom:* I was running a household, catering the local Democratic Party, being everything to everybody. Here I am enrolling my son Dan in school. I had a wonderful time, but there were moments when I felt there was probably something more to life and I just didn't know what it was.

4

5

7

Left: From outings to Easter egg hunts, I am always ready to create an extravaganza. And I do love kids. *Above:* Lieutenant Governor Bill Hobby is a good friend. He had none of this "me Tarzan, you Jane" way about him. Hobby was the first man outside my immediate circle of friends who ever talked to me as if we were on an equal footing. *Right:* Here I am on a cold morning in Plainview, Texas, at Billy Clayton's pheasant hunt.

8

Left: I introduced Geraldine Ferraro at a big rally on the state capitol steps. People liked her. My opening remarks were, essentially, "People ask me all the time, will Texans vote for a woman? Well, my Mama didn't call me Bubba!" *Below:* Fritz Mondale and his staff invited me and about thirty other women to discuss his vice-presidential choice. You can't imagine how thrilling it was to have a nominee for president seriously seeking the advice of women.

11

12

Top: Barbara Jordan's keynote address was so substantive, so powerful. What did I have to say? *Bottom:* I wish Dukakis/Bentsen would have won. But the suggestion that somehow the Democratic party is dead because it doesn't run the presidency, when it wins most of the elections in the country, is dead wrong.

13

14

Above: During my keynote address at the Democratic National Convention, the crowd went crazy when Ginger Rogers did it backwards and in high heels. That's the joy of saying what you actually think in public; anything that comes out of your mouth is really yours. *Left:* We can talk all we want about concepts and ideas, but basically what we want is a future that is good for our grandchildren. This is my granddaughter Lily.

David was paired up in a canoe with his friend Wayne, who was a hypochondriac to begin with and never traveled without his guitar or his considerable satchel of pills. Early the first day they capsized and lost both the guitar and the pills. Somehow, through miraculous scrambling, they had saved the food. They were really looking forward to our epicurean fixings.

When they opened the first morning's breakfast packet they found a can of Metrecal chili, a can of dietetic lima beans, a carrot, and a can of Right Guard spray deodorant. Maybe, they figured, the deodorant was a metaphor.

For lunch they found Sego tuna-noodle casserole, a sack of dried apricots, and a box of Tampax. Odd. But the river awaited.

When they put in for the night they set up camp, made a fire, and opened the third packet. They found a raw potato, a can of beets, a box of prunes, and a sack of Massengill Douche Powder. We had timed it perfectly; when it finally dawned on them what we had done they were way downriver, no way to turn back.

But hope springs eternal. In the morning, thinking perhaps "They wouldn't do this to us for the entire three days," they opened the breakfast pouch. Wayne threw the can of dietetic peas as far into the woods as he could fling it. He turned to my husband and said, "David, do you think Ann is unhappy about your taking this trip?"

As I have no doubt made clear, from outings to Easter egg hunts I am always ready to create an extravaganza. One December day before Christmas I had gone to lunch with one of my closest friends and fellow political activist, Betty McKool. We had read in the paper that they were having the Dallas Antique Show, a mammoth affair, out at Fair Park and we thought we would go have a look.

We got out there and there were hundreds of tables piled

with odd stuff, some of it valuable, some of it incredible junk. At one booth a cluster of old spectacles caught our eye. One pair had lenses so thick it made Betty look like Mr. Magoo, another was a pince-nez that pinched on the end of my nose and was connected by a little chain to a lapel pin. There was a spring in this pin, and when you tugged at it the glasses would fly back into the holder.

We tried on these glasses and started laughing, we thought we were the funniest things. And really, we were, so we bought them.

Usually gags like that wear thin pretty quickly. But we kept putting the glasses on and laughing about how funny we were, and we thought we should have our picture made, me in the pince-nez and Betty in her magnifying glasses. But you know, we told each other, it's not good just to have our pictures taken in these things, we have to dress for the occasion.

In my house I always kept an enormous box of dress-ups. The kids played dress-up all the time and the box was always there if you wanted to put together some kind of costume. So we commenced to dress the part. I gathered a full skirt and an old mutton-sleeved blouse, and stuffed my bosom so I looked sort of like an old dowager. Betty found a short little girl's dress and some fake Shirley Temple curls. We were a pair.

Betty's husband, Mike, practiced condemnation law; if the government condemned your land for a public purpose, Mike represented you to get you as much money as he could. Part of his presentation was pictures, and his law firm had a photographer on call. We called him

In some enlightened moment David and I had acquired a large sign saying "Temperance." We had stumbled on it in one of our travels and found it amusing. Our testament to Temperance was at that very moment sitting in the backyard. Betty and I decided that it would be our backdrop.

The photographer knocked. He was used to shooting

condemned property, so he was kind of surprised when this dowager club woman in a pince-nez greeted him at the door. "I'm from Mr. McKool's office," he said. Betty put him right at ease. "I'm Mrs. McKool." She was a suspiciously aged school-girl. "We're gonna get our picture made." He must have thought we were both crazy, and we probably were.

We took the photographs and got them back and they were hysterical. They were too good not to share, so we got the notion of sending them to our friends for Christmas. We went down to the local photo store where people usually took their children's pictures and family portraits to be turned into re-membrances and had a bunch of these cards made up. On the outside it had little birds, little birdhouses, with the lovely sentiment, "From our house to your house." On the inside we inserted a printed card that said, "Extremism in the pursuit of a Merry Christmas is no vice." Barry Goldwater could not have put it better. We stuck this card into the place usually slotted for the photograph, and placed the photo underneath it, so that you had to remove the card to see who it was.

We mailed these to a lot of people, maybe a hundred, and we didn't sign them. And we had such a good time thinking about people getting this weird card and trying to figure out who it could possibly be from, thinking maybe it was their wives' relatives. Oh, we laughed about that. And we kept thinking of some guy opening it and drawling, "Mildred come here, look at this card we got in the mail."

No more than half our friends recognized us, maybe not that many.

This Christmas card became a tradition. Every year Betty and I came up with some goofy dress-up and made a card out of it. And every year the planning got more elaborate and took lots and lots of time. I mean, we did some that were posters.

One of my favorites was when we hung a bunch of stuffed deer heads, like you see on the wall of a lodge, and cut holes where we could stick our heads through and put on these antlers. And the message was, "If you think I'm gonna pull that damned old sleigh one more year . . ."

Probably the best card artistically was the one that read, in huge red Gothic letters "Hark!" You opened it up and there was the manger my son Dan had built. And in that manger Betty and I sat in a Nativity scene, backlit, a solemn crèche, with me dressed up as Joseph and Betty as Mary. We were both surprised and grinning. And the legend read, "It's a girl!"

One year I dressed up as Dolly Parton, full of exaggeration, and Betty was Wonder Woman. Another year we donned cowboy hats and glittering western wear, and sent "Greetings from the Rhinestone Cow Chips."

Another Christmas Betty was dressed as an elf and I was dressed as Santa Claus, and we shot the photograph in a stable. The front of the card read, "Let me make one thing perfectly clear . . ." (This was obviously during the Nixon years between 1968 and '74.) The insert card said, "You're getting the same thing for Christmas you've been getting all year." And when you took out the picture there I was as Santa standing in front of this horse's rear end, and Betty was shoveling something large and clumpy into a bag.

That year we got back from the photo session just in time to have to drive someone home from my house. There wasn't time to change out of our costumes, and we wouldn't have changed if there had been. Santa and his elf were going for a drive. We ran into all sorts of people, turned some heads. Workers would stare and laugh, and I'd lean out the window and talk with them, ask them what they wanted for Christmas. We had the holiday spirit.

And through it all, every year in each of the photographs, Betty wore her Magoos and I wore my pince-nez.

We had a hit on our hands. People would get their feelings

hurt if they didn't receive our card. I'd get these calls saying, "Ann, is something wrong? Are we not friends anymore? I haven't gotten my card this year."

Our Christmas photo album lasted nine years. By the time we quit doing it the mailing list was up to five hundred people.

8

★

IN 1969 David and I decided to leave Dallas. David wanted to make a change, but we couldn't decide where to go. You always say to yourself, "Before I quit my job I have to know what I'm going to do." I didn't think that made sense. I thought we could make two decisions. The first decision was: we are going to move. Once you make that decision you can make the second, which is: what I am going to do.

We considered going to San Antonio and Corpus Christi; we liked both of those towns very much. But we really both wanted to live in Austin. Our friends Sam and Virginia Whitten had moved there some time before and we missed them desperately. We'd started making mini-treks to Austin on the weekends to see them, and oh, how they must have dreaded seeing us come. We'd drive up Friday night, unload the four kids, spend the night in sleeping bags all over their house. After a jillion trips, we headed there for good. David would practice law with Sam Houston Clinton and I would bring up the kids.

Austin has a big heart. There is an ambiance there that allows you to be whoever you want to be and do whatever you want to do, and the people of Austin will respect your right to do that. It has always been progressive in its attitude.

A lot of Southern towns and Texas towns have a pretty rigid social structure, but not Austin, partially because it is the state capital, and the Texas legislature, for good or ill, comes in and out every two years. The elected officials change from time to time, so there's something of an ebb and flow. It's a fluid community and has never gotten set in its ways because so many of the people there are young. The university brings in new students and visiting professors, and plays, music, dance.

In Austin, if you choose to make your debut, to be a part of the social strata, that's all right. And if you choose to be a part of the hippie community, that's all right too. I have never flown home to Austin that I wasn't glad to be there.

In Dallas, Dan had never been able to have a dog that didn't get run over. We lived on such a very busy street. So the big question was, Can we find a place where Dan can have a dog? That's all he cared about. I looked everywhere for a house and couldn't find anything we could afford. Finally I stumbled on a house out on Red Bud Trail in West Lake Hills that had been built by a doctor many years before as a weekend retreat. It was on a couple of acres of land and as soon as I saw it I knew I didn't want to live anywhere else.

When you stood out on the house's little balcony you saw the lights of North Austin. The house faced out over a canyon called Oracle Gorge, so named because if you stood and stared down into it long enough, the answers would come.

The house was definitely too small for us but there was no question we had to buy it. We packed our belongings into the car, looking like junk dealers, and moved in. The first night we slept on bedrolls in the living room because our furniture hadn't arrived, and Clark looked out over the town and said, "Mama, it's like a garden of lights."

We had to add on to the house right away. I had an architect come out and draw up some preliminary plans, but then he got another job and I found a man named John Huber, one of the world's originals. I sat down with John, who had built a number of houses in his life, and showed him on a piece of paper what I wanted to do. He said, "Oh, don't worry about it, we don't need an architect. We'll just build it."

I liked to hear that. It wasn't as brave as Mama going to town and getting day help, but it was close. John would arrive in the morning and say, "Well, what do you think we ought to do today?" And I'd say, "Well, I don't know, why don't we knock out the living room wall and start there."

We lived in that house, with canvas sheeting covering gaping holes from the second story to the ground, for months. We built a bedroom and a bath for David and me, and a great big living room with a vaulted ceiling and tiled floors, and a huge screened porch. We doubled the house's square footage. It was a very big project and it took a lot of my time.

When it got done it was really a home. And it was always filled with people. We were glad to be back with Sam and Virginia and their children. We met Mike and Sue Sharlot, Bob and Dagmar Hamilton, Toni and Bob Palter. That house was a wonderful place. I think of it as lots of music and lots of people laughing.

When I left Dallas, I promised myself I would never have anything to do with politics again. It was like when I went to high school and was going to be the new me. Women, it was painfully clear, weren't going to be allowed to use their brains and I certainly wanted to use mine. I didn't see politics as producing anything fruitful for me. My kids were school age, which meant I could get out of the house more often, and I saw this as an opportunity to go back to the university and take some courses, learn some new things.

The same year we moved to Austin, David argued his first case before the United States Supreme Court. It was a free-

speech case involving a Dallas alternative newspaper called
Notes from the Underground, which was being raided by the
Dallas police. The law-enforcement officials insisted the raids
were because of the paper's alleged obscenity, but David argued
they were a pretext to censor *Notes's* anti–Vietnam War editorial positions.

You cannot sleep in the Supreme Court. I know, because
I had Dan and Cecile with me and one particularly vigilant
usher kept signaling me every time Dan's head hit my shoulder.
Dan was all of ten years old at the time, but in the Supreme
Court they are sticklers for the rules.

David won his case and we were all thrilled. He went back
to argue two single-member district cases in the early seventies,
gerrymandering cases that were landmark decisions and dramatically changed Texas politics. David never really worked in
a campaign; he was the thinker, the philosopher. These vic-
tories added greatly to the ability of blacks and Hispanics to
make races for local offices.

Meanwhile, I was cooking, tending to the kids, hosting
parties. The first couple of years on Red Bud Trail in Austin I
was kind of getting my feet on the ground and helping the kids
get theirs. It was particularly hard on Cecile, because she was
older and she was shy, and what with the move to a new city,
new neighborhood, new school, it was a difficult time for her
to make friends. I was a Mom, that's what I was involved in.

I got involved with our neighborhood, serving on the local
zoning and planning commission. I learned that people take
their property very seriously, and that it was a real tightrope
walk trying to keep property owners' interests in balance with
the overall good of the community. It was next to impossible
to keep people satisfied.

One day in late 1971, two years after we had arrived in
Austin, I got a call from a woman named Carol Yontz. She
wanted me to have lunch with a young woman who wanted to

run for the Texas legislature. I carefully explained to her that I was not involved in politics, I wasn't going to do that anymore, that I had other interests that I wanted to pursue. Carol said, "Just come and talk with her. Just visit with her. We really do need advice. Her name is Sarah Weddington."

I had seen Sarah Weddington's name in the newspaper; she was the woman who argued *Roe* vs. *Wade* before the Supreme Court. Somehow I had the impression that she was an older woman, in her late fifties or sixties. I thought I was dealing with some old-guard progressive whom I simply had never run across.

I went to lunch and was stunned to meet a very attractive young woman, twenty-five years old, with lots of curly blond hair, who was all business. She wanted to run for the Texas legislature but had been unable to find any man with practical experience in politics who would agree to help her. Her husband was all for it; they practiced law together, but professional politics was run by men and there were no men willing to take her on.

She said to me, "I really want to serve in the Texas legislature; there are a number of laws that need correction." She wanted legislation giving a woman the right to credit in her own name and not her husband's. She wanted laws that would stop the practice of putting the woman rape victim on trial for her character rather than the assailant on trial for his assault. She wanted to make it illegal to fire a teacher because of pregnancy.

But the main issue of the campaign seemed to boil down to the fact that Sarah was a woman. Government, to that point, hadn't been women's work. She had to convince Travis County that she was up to it, and she was running against two men.

What impressed me about Sarah Weddington was that she was pretty and feminine, and yet she talked about really tough issues involving women—and she made sense. She was not threatening to the men we interviewed. I don't think I had been around any women who I would call out-and-out feminist activists until I met Sarah. She had absolutely no concrete political experience, didn't know how to organize a campaign, project an image, or get voters to the polls. All she knew was that she wanted to get to the legislature and fight for good laws. I listened to her talk and I was really taken by the fact that she, at that age, was willing to carry on this kind of pursuit.

I agreed I would help her. I was about ten years older than Sarah and the group of aides and helpers in her campaign, and Sarah in essence agreed that she would listen to what I had to say and then do what I told her to do.

I don't mean to suggest that I ran the whole campaign, because it really was a cooperative effort. Sarah's husband, Ron Weddington, and Carol Yontz had a big part in directing the effort. But all the same, this was the first time I had had a candidate come to me and willingly listen seriously to anything I had to say about what to do.

I don't want you to think I was down there pointing my finger and cracking a whip, because it wasn't that way. We encouraged cooperation in that organization, and, being women, we were more apt to give and get than the people in other Democratic campaigns in which I had worked. Our problem, if anything, was volunteers: how to find enough things for all of them to do.

Women were coming out of kitchens all over Austin to get involved; the fact that Sarah was making this race was a very dramatic step.

Sarah's campaign was run out of her law office. I still had the kids to handle and the house to run, but I would go into town every day and we would review what was to be done. My role largely involved coaching Sarah on how to act, how to carry herself, how to respond to questions. Once, when we went to a Rotary Club luncheon, Sarah was asked, "What do you think about flat-track betting?" She thought he was talking about mattresses and sheets; I had to explain to her quietly that he was talking about horse race gambling.

Most people, when they think of political campaigns, have a romantic notion that the candidate and his or her advisers sit and wrestle with issues. What they usually sit and wrestle with is how to save money, how to get something done for cheap. Sarah's campaign was that in spades.

At one point we literally ran out of money. We didn't start with much and not a whole lot ever came our way, and during one of our lowest moments a big Democratic rally was about to be held where each of the candidates could set up a booth, hand out literature, make their biggest impact. We didn't have enough money for the booth, and if they gave us the booth we didn't have anything to give away.

Somehow we scrounged up the dollars to reserve the space, but the fixings were beyond us. I thought long and hard about how we could get Sarah's name around. Finally it dawned on me that all of these people who were going around picking up pencils and emery boards and brochures with all the other candidates' names on them would need something to put the stuff in.

We called a friend, Vic Ravel. Vic and his wife Myra were good Democrats, and he ran a paper company. We asked Vic if he would donate some shopping bags to the cause. Paper sacks. We had a bunch of bumper stickers, so we took the bumper stickers and stuck them onto our free sacks, and when people struggled by laden down with other candidates' freebies we handed them a Sarah Sack to put it all in.

There was such a clamor for these Sarah Sacks that we ran out of bumper stickers. We still had a good supply of sacks, though, so some of the campaign workers and I sat in the back of the booth and wrote "Sarah Weddington" in longhand across the face of the bags and started handing them out. When word got out that we had "autographed Sarah Sacks," people just came in droves.

Sarah Weddington's candidacy greatly benefited from the gubernatorial candidacy of Sissy Farenthold, who was running at the same time. Ben Barnes, the lieutenant governor, was getting bad press suggesting that he was part of the Sharpstown Scandal, and the race was thrown wide open.

The Sharpstown Scandal read like a *Who's Who* of public officials. Essentially, the suggestion was that officeholders and others had benefited from sweetheart loans to purchase stock in the National Bankers Life Insurance Company, manipulated by a Houston banker/real estate developer/businessman named Frank Sharp. The stock price was inflated, it was alleged; stock purchases, sales, and transactions were arranged like a maze, and some of the sellers reaped the benefits of a large scam.

Governor Preston Smith, Democratic Party Chairman Elmer Baum, House Speaker Gus Mutscher, and others purchased and later sold the NBL stock. Attorney General Waggoner Carr was one of the principal owners of National Bankers Life. Only Gus Mutscher and two of his friends were tried and convicted, but the stories were in the headlines for months, and all the political people involved lost their races the next year.

Although later stories revealed that he was not involved, Ben Barnes came out the greatest loser. He was the heir apparent to Governor John Connally and had announced his own candidacy for governor, but the continuing Sharpstown controversy added fuel to Sissy Farenthold's run.

There had been a revolt of sorts in the Texas House of Representatives, and thirty state legislators, known affectionately as the "Dirty Thirty," had banded together to try to reform the House, reduce the control of the speaker, democratize committee assignments, and move along legislation. Sissy had been a leader of the "Dirty Thirty."

Women and progressives flocked to Sissy's candidacy, it

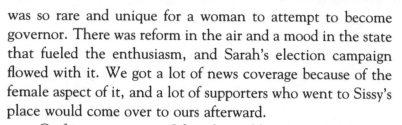

was so rare and unique for a woman to attempt to become governor. There was reform in the air and a mood in the state that fueled the enthusiasm, and Sarah's election campaign flowed with it. We got a lot of news coverage because of the female aspect of it, and a lot of supporters who went to Sissy's place would come over to ours afterward.

Crafting a campaign, I found, was like accomplishing any other project; you have to determine who can give you what you need to win. And the key to success is finding your allies. In Sarah's race we had to seek out those people who would naturally be our friends, among them environmentalists, women, blacks, Hispanics, students.

I felt then and feel now that minorities and women are natural allies. Not only minorities but schoolteachers, farmers, young people . . . anyone outside the power structure. What has held us back has not been the lack of talent or brains, it has been the lack of education and opportunity. We can't win if we can't play. The main thing that has held us all back is ignorance and prejudice, and they stem from the same source. Anyone who will make disparaging remarks about blacks or Hispanics or Asians, will make disparaging remarks about women too. If it happens to be a woman, then she's a fool.

Anti–Vietnam War activism was becoming strong at the time and the University of Texas campus was alive with political awareness. This was part of Sarah's natural constituency.

This was the first time I really became aware of Mary Beth Rogers, although her mother, Anita Coniglio, had been my friend in Dallas. She was working on the campaign and she had a sense of marketing that far exceeded anyone else's. We knew that the largest single body of employees in Austin was the University of Texas non-teaching staff, and that they had not received a pay raise in years. Mary Beth designed a postcard on purple stock that said, "You have not been treated fairly. You haven't had a raise in years. Vote for Sarah Weddington."

We organized the volunteers to go through the UT directory and weed out everyone but the non-teaching staff, then we directed our mail to those who were left.

That was pretty revolutionary stuff for a local campaign. Usually you mail clubs and organizations, things with mailing lists. Here we'd created our own.

We looked inside these voting groups for issues where Sarah felt comfortable and those she could do something about once she got elected. Historic preservation was important to Austinites; clean air and water cut across all lines; carefully planned highways served everyone. All of these issues affect neighborhood groups in the present and the future.

But elections are won by more than issues. In fact, issues are often not at the top of the list. People will very definitely align themselves on a long issue line, but by and large I firmly believe that they vote for people they trust.

Most of us don't expect candidates or elected officials to think exactly as we think on every issue. It would be impossible. What we do want is someone who has balance, someone we believe has judgment, and someone who seriously cares about us. Sarah was all of that. She was warm and compassionate. Plus, in the field she was a high-quality performer, she thought well on her feet, and she looked good on television.

I was truly excited to take on this challenge, with the issue very clearly being whether a woman could do this job or not. I was stimulated by the opportunities to go places and have a forum and speak in a way that seemed productive. I had participated in marches before, protests, demonstrations. But this time we went and, whether they wanted you there or not, they heard you once you came. Or, they heard Sarah.

This was also the first action I'd taken in my adult life that

I'd done on my own. David had been involved in the campaign, but he'd been involved because I was involved, rather than the other way around. If there was any significance for me personally, that was it.

I loved working in that campaign because of the general good feeling among the people who were in on it. It was not as it had been in Dallas, where someone told you where to go and what to do. This was a group of people who would talk through problems together and decide how to deal with them. I'd never been exposed to that kind of decision-making.

We came out of the primary and had a runoff against a man named Hugh Hornsby. Hornsby complained that Sarah was trying to confuse the voters; one day she would wear her hair up, the next day she would wear her hair down. That caused a certain amount of laughter. But Hugh Hornsby was serious, and the question of whether a woman could do the job as Texas legislator was seriously asked. It was the central issue of the campaign.

No one could have been more surprised than I that we won.

The nice thing for me was that Sarah went to the Texas House of Representatives to serve and I went home. That's what I liked best. I loved the crafting and figuring out how to put it all together, how to get it done on election day. And then I got to go home to the real world.

My retirement didn't last long. After one session of the legislature, Carol Yontz, Sarah's original administrative assistant, left to take a job in Washington and in 1974 Sarah asked me to take her place. Well, by then the kids were in school and there didn't seem any reason for me not to do it. I made one stipulation: I had to set my own hours. I would certainly give Sarah Weddington her money's worth, but I had to have some flexibility. If I needed to leave work to come home or to deal with one of the kids in school, she must understand that I was going to do that; my family came first. Sarah was agreeable, so I came on board.

I worked for Sarah for one legislative session. At one time I was managing five interns from the LBJ School, plus a secretary and a receptionist, and we were all in two very small rooms. I got to know firsthand how the Texas House of Representatives works, I got a deeper and more realistic understanding than I'd ever had of real-world politics: how bills become law, how to deal with constituents' problems. I drafted all of Sarah's correspondence, helped lay out a legislative package, planned with her what she was going to do in the session, and hired staff to help track those bills through.

Sarah was very good, very well-organized, and she had a way about her that I still envy. Sarah could get people to do things that would be helpful to her, and all the while she was bending people to her will she would be consistently charming about it.

It was while I was working for Sarah that I first got to know Bill Hobby. He was lieutenant governor, and he was the first man outside my immediate circle of friends who ever talked to me as if we were on equal footing. He had none of this "I'm-experienced-and-you're-not," "Me Tarzan, you Jane" way about him. I was really taken with his easy manner and his extraordinary kindness.

But running Sarah's office was my job, not my life. My life was with my family. I was really involved with my kids' PTA, school board meetings, gardens, and pets.

I realize, as I tell all this, that what seems to be of merit or significance about what I've done in life hinges around activity that one ordinarily would see men doing. There I was, living this incredibly active life that was bits and pieces stitched together, and those pieces that were female activity don't seem worth telling about.

What little girls read in history books or are assigned papers to write on, is always about men and what men do; there is little or no history written about women and what women do. The obvious result is that, as we live our lives, we have to make things up as we go along. It's as if each woman has to create her own solutions.

I want to describe the female side of my life, which certainly occupied ninety percent of my time and attention, but it's difficult to tell the story.

Managing a very complex household, providing nurturing and caring and encouragement for the children, is a hard, hard job. I learned more about management from running a household than I have from any other single occupation.

Perhaps it would be the same with a man who was running a major corporation; he could talk about the meetings of the board and the decisions that were made there, and the sessions that took place, because the end result would have had some major impact on international commerce. We have millions of board meetings in our lives, they just happen to consist of a husband and wife and their children and friends. And the consequences are also major; they have a direct impact on human life and what will happen to each of these people individually.

When women's board meetings are over, however, we jump into the car and go do the Christmas shopping, or pick up whoever it was that was left at the ballet lesson. Somebody is sick down the street; you take them a pot of chicken soup. Someone needs help with their homework, you're the expert. It isn't as though you go through a really tough day and at five or six or seven o'clock it's over, because it isn't.

It's an enormous job, and yet we are given very little training for it. Suddenly we have babies and we are supposed to be "good mothers," without ever having been schooled in it. It's supposed to be some instinctive ability. So we devour every book in sight about babies, and of course the books

146

change dramatically from one generation to the next so you never know whether or not what your mother did was right, what you are doing is right, or what your daughter does will be right.

I think most women are scared to death, because we are molding and influencing the most important thing we have ever created, our children. So here we are, sailing out into these totally uncharted waters. And for someone like me, who was trying and wanting to be the very best at everything, there were a lot of anxious, anxious moments.

Most women are not fighters, we weren't brought up to fight, fighting comes unnaturally to us. Little boys are encouraged to stand up for themselves; little girls are told to keep their dresses clean and reason things out. As a result, we are very good negotiators. We know almost instinctively that if everyone can leave the table saving face, the outcome is going to be more satisfactory to everyone.

My daughter Cecile was a model child. She was the one David and I, in our youthful earnestness, insisted on teaching all the rules. None of this left-alone, free-thinking upbringing. As with all first children, she got the full brunt of our inexperience. So I was shocked one morning when I got a call at home saying that Cecile had been asked to leave school. If it had been one of the boys I would have thought nothing of it, but with Cecile it was just extraordinary.

The principal was on the phone and I said, "You must be making a mistake."

He said, "Indeed not. She will have to leave school immediately."

"What in the world has she done?"

"She wore a black arm band to school this morning."

It was the middle of the Vietnam War and this had been a day of national protest, and the school was having none of this Free Speech nonsense.

———————— ★ ————————

When I got there I told Cecile not to worry, and then I pitched a fit.

This was the public school system and the school board was always making these demands for blind devotion, and I was up in arms. It seemed to be my task in the struggle. Kids were being denied the right to go to their own commencement ceremonies because they were wearing long hair. The school system cut out teaching all languages but English and Spanish because they were low on funds; Cecile was studying German and I was incensed that she would be denied a language while there were plenty of frivolous courses being offered.

They were forming a pep squad in Cecile's high school, the kind where girls wear short skirts and pom-poms and jump and twirl in the cause of school spirit. I think they were called the Hi-Lines. Cecile brought home a sheet of paper announcing the formation of this prestigious organization and the requirements for membership. You couldn't be over a certain height or a certain weight, and Cecile didn't fit.

Well, the top of my head came off. This school was taking my tax dollars, public monies, and putting them into activities that were going to be denied my daughter because she was an inch too tall! What kind of a system is that? I was outraged and got on the phone and complained loudly.

About the same time, Dan came home really excited because his gym class had been given Gatorade as a reward for cleaning out the varsity football players' lockers. Dan was in junior high and, of course, thought it was a wonderful honor.

"Son," I asked, "why can't the football boys clean out their own lockers?"

The football boys were too busy, they had to practice.

Again, I got exercised. The message being sent was unpleasant: "These guys are the nuts, you lesser little kids can pick up after them." I was so angry I didn't know what to do.

I ended up taking my kids out of the public school system

and enrolling them in St. Stephen's, an Episcopal school. For starters, St. Stephen's was integrated, while the Eanes school district where my kids had been going was still all-white. I am one of the great believers in the public school system, and as a philosophical matter it bothers me deep down that my kids did not graduate from the public schools.

All this sounds like political activity, but it wasn't; it was just dealing with the everyday activity of my kids. I was a volunteer at the elementary school library, and at least once a week I would go and read stories to the children, and design and decorate the bulletin boards. That seems like a small chore, but it took an awful lot of time and I did it for several years.

There were plenty of other things going on. We had a greenhouse built off the garage, and Virginia Whitten and I were deep into organic vegetables, mulching and composting. There was an infestation of pill bugs, and I pulled out an organic garden magazine, which told me to do things like put out pans of beer and the pill bugs would crawl in them and die. Minimally successful.

The piece of advice that did work was the one about the grapefruits. We turned grapefruit halves upside down and the pill bugs would crawl into the grapefruit half and get stuck and die, and then we'd throw them away. We called them Grapefruit Motels.

My son Clark had a little trouble in school. He was in second grade and the principal called and told me that Clark was a discipline problem. Now, Clark was such a good little boy that I couldn't figure it out. When he came home I asked him what was going on.

"Mama," he said, "the teacher can't get everybody quiet." Apparently she couldn't get control of the class; kids just walked up and around and down by Clark's desk, and he couldn't stand it. He was going crazy with all the mayhem, and when it got overwhelming for him he would bang his head on his desk until the teacher sent him out of the room. All the principal saw was this little boy banging his head against the desk.

I said, "Okay, Clark, let's make a deal. I'm going to take you to school early tomorrow and I want you to go straight to the library and get a book that you would like to read. Then I want you to see if the teacher will let you sit somewhere else. If you can, sit in the back of the room and make a list of all your homework and read that library book. Do not bang your head on your desk, and do not cause a ruckus with any of the kids."

We had a deal.

Three days later the teacher called. "Clark has a problem."

"What is it now?"

"He is reading library books in class."

If it hadn't been my son I'd have gotten a kick out of this.

"Is he doing his work?" I asked.

"Well, yes, he's doing his work, but he doesn't do it in class."

"Why do you care where he does it?"

"I would like for him to participate with the other children."

I thought about pounding my head against my desk.

"If he's doing his homework and he's doing his classwork," I said as gently as I could, "let's just let him read that library book, okay?"

Ellen, our youngest, was an amazing child. Perhaps all children with three older siblings are self-sufficient, but Ellen not only took care of herself, she knew where everything was that belonged to any of the rest of us. She knew where everyone was, at baseball practice or piano lessons, and could handle the telephone like an executive secretary. Ellen always said whatever was on her mind. Early on she'd be sitting in a loaded grocery cart, point a stubby finger at a woman in line and say,

"Your hair sure is funny-looking." I would just crack right up.

Myself, I was certainly a picture of perpetual motion. And most of the things I did, I did well; for me, that was the point. But I was feeling my way along. Keeping a household fairly clean and attractive and decorated, putting good food on the table, getting children delivered to the various places they needed to be; fighting the battle of the PTA or the school board, being involved peripherally in political races, volunteering at school, being room mother—I mean, you have here a tossed salad that's bigger than most bowls. I have always felt that I was holding on to a horse running pell-mell. And I am the horse.

In 1974 I was contacted by Charles Miles, a black friend who had supported and campaigned for Sarah Weddington. Charles called and asked whether I might come over and help out on Wilhelmina Delco's campaign to become the first black to represent Austin in the Texas legislature. I was happy to do it, but Wilhelmina was so good she didn't need much help. Discriminatory laws, higher education for blacks, public school issues, teenage pregnancy—these were the things she knew backward and forward. It is amazing how everything changes but everything stays the same.

Wilhelmina was experienced, she had served on the school board, had a network and record of her own. She had qualifications; she didn't need to be created from scratch. Her main problem was the turf fights that were going on at her own headquarters. I was brought in as some sort of expert, having just been successful turning Sarah from an attorney into an officeholder, but mostly I helped with strategy and introductions.

When Wilhelmina won, she became the first black, man or woman, to be elected to the legislature from Travis County.

Richard Moya had made a breakthrough in the Hispanic

community and was serving on the County Commissioner's Court. (Richard claims he developed his organization from playing in the city softball league.) That same year, Gonzalo Barrientos ran for the Texas House and I went over and worked in his headquarters. He had run in 1972 and lost, but was successful in his second try.

In the spring of 1975 a group of people approached David about running in the Democratic primary for the post of county commissioner. There was a fellow named Johnny Voudouris who had been in office for three terms, going on twelve years, and the general drift was that Voudouris was just not doing all that good a job. With Sarah's campaign, and Wilhelmina's and Gonzalo's, and some progressive organizing, there was an effort to begin a grass-roots movement to bring in loyal Democrats on a local level.

David decided that he didn't want to run. The truth of the matter is that David would probably have made a superb officeholder, but he would have made a rotten candidate. He didn't have the patience, it simply wasn't in his nature. Being a candidate for office requires a certain doggedness at doing mundane things. What the public sees is all the hype and the flash, the television advertisements, the radio spots, all of that public dancing. They don't see the tedium of planning organizational efforts, of slogging from one small meeting to another small meeting, of designing and printing and paying for the brochures. (We're talking about races where you don't have the money to hire the professional help that does those things; only the bigger, glamorous races have that.)

Running for office requires going to visit every single organization that invites you to make a speech, because if you don't they think you don't like them or are not on their side. It means that night after night after night you're out making appearances, sometimes going to three or four events in one evening. Even if you're not making a speech you'll go by and shake hands and make an impression. Shaking and howdying. It's very, very hard work, and there is no immediate gratification. Usually you'll start these things months or years ahead, and election day is the gratification. If you win.

David does not suffer fools easily, and while there are a lot of really wonderful and well-intentioned people out there, there are also a lot who think the campaign is going to rise and fall on their particular issue. In a local election there may be an issue that doesn't affect more than literally two dozen people, but because it is important to them it is a big thing. So a candidate has to be long on listening, long on understanding, and long on patience. I am surprised more mothers haven't ventured into electoral politics.

When David declined, they approached me.

I had never wanted to serve in public office. I had spent a little time on the zoning and planning commission and I knew what that was like; you couldn't make anyone happy. At the end of a campaign I had always felt a tremendous relief; I'd had the fun part, the figuring and conceiving and strategizing; now poor Sarah or Wilhelmina had to serve.

And I had seen the personal toll it took on them. I knew that, if you are good at it, running for office takes your total involvement, total interest.

Plus, I really thought it was pretty far out to think that a woman could run for county commissioner. It's perceived as a truck-driving, front-end-loader operation, taking care of the roads.

County commissioners are those elected officials between the level of city and state government. They were the established governmental unit before there were cities to govern. It is the level at which most Texas judicial proceedings take place. If you are going to court, you are going to go to the county courthouse, where the county commissioners are the executive body.

In Texas, by constitution, there are four commissioners and one judge, who is the presiding officer of the Commissioner's Court, even though that judge may not have judicial responsibilities in the ordinary sense. Counties are divided into four precincts, and the commissioners define the boundaries.

The Commissioner's Court establishes the budget and tax rate for the county, and builds and maintains the county jails. It funds all of the functions of county government, including rural roads and bridges, transportation planning, voter registration, county parks, juvenile and adult probation, the tax assessor collector's office, the sheriff's office, the entire law enforcement area, and all of the judges. It determines how much money is going to be spent in each department and literally draws the budget to govern the county operations.

The county government is also the level on which a number of human service projects are funded; it is pretty much within the bailiwick of the Commissioner's Court to determine what shall and shall not be funded in human service affairs. Welfare, food stamps—it's all under the county commissioners. Texas was not noticeably hospitable to the notion that a woman could handle that kind of responsibility, so when I was approached to run it seemed like a farfetched idea.

And, in truth, I was afraid that if I ran for public office and I was successful and served, it would be the end of my marriage.

It's different for women in office than it is for men. Women have the primary responsibility for the household, for raising the children, and for getting the meals on the table. I don't care how much things change, or how much men say "I'm going to be a helpmate and I want somebody who is going to be independent and responsible." The truth of the matter is, men expect somebody to put food on the table for them, to provide for all of those little things that keep life together. That's all there is to it.

Now, I'm just saying this as a general rule. I know there are exceptions, and that there are men who do the laundry and who go to the grocery store and plan the meals. But most of the men I know go to the grocery store with a list of instructions. And that list is put together by the female of the household. Men drive the car pool or pick up the cleaning because they are told to, not because they wake up that morning and say, "Gee, I need to go to the cleaners and get our cleaning." So, if a woman is not there, the whole management of the house suffers.

I don't know very many men who plan their household's social life. By and large they go and do whatever the female of the household has planned. It's the same way with the children; I don't know very many fathers who plan the birthday parties or see to it that the cake gets baked and the ice cream gets bought. They may pick it up when they are asked to, but they don't plan it.

I wanted to be, and I was, everything to everybody. I believed all of the magazine articles extolling how wonderful we are—the front page of *Family Circle, Good Housekeeping*—how we are the decorators and chauffeurs and nurses and chefs and social planners.

Well, campaigning for public office, serving in public office, or for that matter working at any really demanding vocation, demands your full-time attention. I had been around enough to see that the kind of campaign you run tells what kind of officeholder you're going to be; you see a lazy, laid-back campaigner, you're going to have a lazy, laid-back officeholder. If I was going to do it, I was going to do it right.

David and I had been married twenty-two years, and change is really threatening to any relationship, particularly marriage. You can weather it, but the dynamic of a relationship is a terribly fragile thing. In my heart of hearts I thought, "If I go off and assume public office and David is left with a lot of the management responsibility of this house, he isn't going to like it very much."

I told them no, I was flattered but I really didn't think I wanted to run.

David told me I was making a mistake.

He said, "Don't do that. Don't tell them no. You will wonder all your life whether you could have done it or not. And in the end, you'll probably be good at it."

I was more than a little surprised. I'm not really sure he knew what he was getting into, and I said so. But he said he knew me, and I believed he did.

The other consideration, the big one in politics, was whether I could win. If I was going to risk such high stakes I wanted to be as certain as I could that this wasn't just a futile gesture. I asked the people who had approached me to pull together statistics that showed the numerical totals of other candidates who had run for office in Travis County. I would make some comparisons, as I would for anybody else who came to me for advice about making a race, and then I would make my decision.

In the previous election a woman named Margaret Hoffman had been elected to the city council. I wanted precinct-by-precinct statistics from those races because Margaret Hoffman's numbers would show me how a female could run there. I wanted the numbers from Gonzalo Barrientos's victory, because that would show me how open each precinct was to a candidate out of the norm, Gonzalo being Hispanic.

A whole bunch of numbers were pulled together and David and I took them and the kids down to South Padre Island. We spent a month at the beach, and we talked and talked and looked at the numbers.

The numbers very clearly said that I could win this race.

David continued to be extremely supportive. "You have given me twenty-two years of your life," he told me, "it's not much to ask for me to give you some years of mine to help run this house and take care of these kids." He became the car pooler and the planner and feeder. And I told them I would run.

We planned a superb campaign. The first thing we did was choose nine target precincts: three which we felt would be very friendly to me, three which would be not-so-friendly, and three which seemed likely to us to be out-and-out hostile. We acquired a list of people who had voted in a recent constitutional-amendment election and those who had voted in a bond election, because if you will vote in that kind of very small and specific election, when the county commissioner is up for grabs you're going to be at the polls come hell or high water. We wanted to concentrate on those people we knew were going to vote.

You hear a lot of candidates tell you, "I knocked on every door in my district." Well, when I hear that, first I know they're not telling me the truth, and second, I know they wasted fifty percent of their time, because half the people don't vote. If you go and knock on every door, you're going to spend a lot of time talking to people who are not going to be at the polls.

I'm a great believer in postcard mailings; you will read a postcard when you won't open a letter. If you get a postcard in your mailbox you will pull it out and look at the other side of it before you drop it in the trash. If it's a color that interests you, you're more likely to read it than if it is white and looks like the rest of the mail. Postcards were our first line of attack.

First we stripped all those names from the voter lists and taped them onto 3 × 5 cards. Then we filed the cards geographically so I could go from one house to another without traipsing back and forth across town twenty times a day. Then we found someone who would drive me to each neighborhood, let me out, drive two blocks, and pick me up. Logistically it involved a great amount of work and time.

We had these postcards designed with my name and picture on one side and a note that said, essentially, "Dear Friend, I'm coming to your neighborhood to talk to you about

157

the issues that I think affect Precinct 3 in Travis County, and about my race for County Commissioner." The cards were mailed about a week before I planned to walk that area, so the prospective voter had heard of me in some fashion before I got to his or her door.

I went only to those houses that were on my 3 × 5 cards, and at each house, if the person was at home, I would give them a brochure and say, "Here is a little something about the county commissioner's race. I'd be happy to talk to you if you are interested." Well, most people don't want to talk to you, but they are glad you came by. And they take your brochure.

After each house I visited, I noted something personal about the conversation and I'd jot it down. If they weren't home I would jot down something about the house itself, maybe a tree house their kids had built in the yard, or if there was a dog. Something they would take personally. Back home I had an identical set of postcards to the ones I'd mailed, but these said, "Dear Friend, I came to your neighborhood to talk to you about the issues." And at night I would write on these postcards, "Your kids have a wonderful tree house," or "You have a great brass door knocker." Those cards stacked up, and we mailed them all at once the week before the election.

That's the way you win elections, through repetitive contact. It can be done by mail, by media, by telephone, or in person. We had three major contacts: two mailings and a visit, plus of course, radio and TV.

It usually works out for the best, but it has its pitfalls. I walked up to one house and the roof was covered with iridescent-feathered pigeons. The entire roof seemed to be moving and cooing. The woman of the house came to the door and I said something about what beautiful pigeons were on her roof. The woman was not pleased.

"Those damn pigeons," she snapped, "I'd like to kill every one of them."

So I was backtracking and switching facial expressions as fast as I could, and I said, "Oh my goodness, is there something wrong with them?"

The woman scowled. "Madeline Murray O'Hare lived one block over, and when she moved she left her damned pigeons in the neighborhood, and they picked me." And of course they proliferated.

I started working the three precincts we had judged to be friendly, but after I visited the first one the feeling was so overwhelmingly positive that I moved immediately to the sort of mid-range, probably-friendly-but-don't-know-for-sure areas. I worked two of them and found the same kind of reception. From there I moved to hostile territory, and while the welcome mats were not always out, it was still very encouraging.

I knew from the statistics that it was going to be hard to convince people outside the city limits that I was their boy. The people directly affected by the county commissioner in a road-blading, water-drainage operation were going to be more resistant to voting for a female than the city folk. But I also knew that these country people consisted of only eleven percent of the vote, so I just didn't campaign there. I figured the odds were too long for such a short payoff, so anything they saw of me they got either on the radio or on television.

My opponent, Johnny Voudouris, was the old-style, good-ol'-boy rural county commissioner. But after more than a decade on the job he had lost touch with what was going on in town. The consistent word I heard, when I asked people at their homes or in public places, was, "Johnny Voudouris won't return my phone call." I paid attention. Anytime you hear a consistent thread among the electorate in a campaign, you'd better look at it; if it's negative, that's a point of vulnerability.

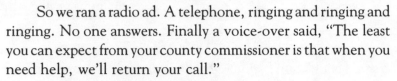

So we ran a radio ad. A telephone, ringing and ringing and ringing. No one answers. Finally a voice-over said, "The least you can expect from your county commissioner is that when you need help, we'll return your call."

But it's not only the voters whom a candidate has to court. There are the movers and the shakers.

I made a list of all the people I felt cared about who the county commissioner was: bank presidents, lawyers, judges, anyone I could think of who could possibly qualify as a "community leader" who might have something directly at stake in the management of the courthouse. I went to see them.

My technique was really very simple. I told them who I was and that I wanted to be county commissioner. Most of them laughed—not a big *ha, ha,* but a sort of smirky amusement. When I got that out of the way I started talking. I didn't ask these people to support me—I wasn't enough of a known quantity; they had too much to lose from Voudouris if they didn't support him and he won. I just said that I would like to have their help if they were inclined to give it.

The real key to those conversations was that I would ask for advice. I'd say, "Tell me what you think. Tell me what I should do, in the campaign and for the precinct." Usually that turned it. If someone asks your opinion, and wants to listen to you, you're always pretty flattered. These men certainly were. And I would always ask if there was anyone else they thought I should see.

When I got home I would follow up these visits with a handwritten note saying, "Thank you for spending time with me. I will follow up on your suggestion . . ." and spell out whatever the specific suggestion had been. Then I would get on the phone and call all the people they had told me I should call. Most of the time these friends would see me, and the circle continued.

I went down to talk to the editorial board of the *Austin*

American-Statesman about an endorsement. The editor was a man named Sam Wood who had been editor of the Waco paper and had known my uncle Jimmie, who had worked as a photographer for the Waco paper in the old days.

I sat down and talked to Sam about what I would do as county commissioner and he looked over at me and said, "Ann, what do you think would happen to this newspaper if we were to endorse you, a woman, for county commissioner?!" I said, "Well, Sam, I don't know. The whole building just might collapse, but why don't you try it and see?"

They endorsed me the following week.

The all-male Austin Headliners Club, made up of men in the general fields of media and journalism, held a stag luncheon each year, and I wanted to make a splash with them. The entertainment that year was Cactus Pryor, a clever, funny man who was Lyndon Johnson's favorite comedian and also ran a radio show that I'd appeared on a number of times. Cactus was a staple at this luncheon and he and his brother Wally were friends of mine. They had invited Johnny Voudouris and me to appear together in one of their skits at the luncheon that year, but when the day came Voudouris didn't show up.

The county has several beautiful parks, and their maintenance is the responsibility of the county commissioners. All of the beautiful parks in Southwest Travis County had trash cans, and on all of the trash cans—stenciled across them in great big letters—was the name: Johnny Voudouris. Well, right before the program began, Wally wheeled out one of these trash cans and set it in the middle of the stage. The men went right on eating and drinking.

There is a tradition of women popping out of things at stag parties, and who was I to challenge tradition? I popped out of that Voudouris trash can, turned it around, and there on the back was one of my bumper stickers. The men just died laughing.

9

★

THE figures didn't lie. My grass-roots organization worked like a dream, and I won. I beat the Republican candidate easily, and I was the new county commissioner of Precinct Three.

I got voter feedback almost immediately. The phone rang one afternoon and when I answered, a woman said, "Mrs. Richards, I have your cat."

I was perplexed. "Yes," I told her, "I have cats. Did one run away?"

"No, Mrs. Richards. You wrote me on that postcard and said if my calico cat ever had kittens, that you wanted one? I have her for you."

David wanted to know what else I had written on those cards that might be coming across our path, and I told him it could be anything. But I went over to the woman's house and got that cat; she turned out to be a darling kitten, and I still have her.

Johnny Voudouris was not pleased about getting beat. When I got to the county commissioner's office he had cleaned it out. I mean, there was not a file in the place. We were starting with nothing.

I had met Jane Hickie in Sarah Weddington's campaign in 1972. A graduate of Mount Holyoke, she was president of the Texas Women's Political Caucus in 1973–74, and traveled all over the state organizing chapters. I thought at the time, and I think today, that Jane was one of the brightest people I had ever met. She had tremendous organizational capabilities, unlimited energy, and real dedication. And she wanted to be a political player. Jane worked like a zealot all through my campaign, and when it was over she came to work for me in the courthouse as my administrative assistant.

If I was active during the campaign, I topped it when I took office. How many times have you heard about a politician who forgot about the people? I wasn't about to be one of them.

When you're an officeholder your work day does not end at a specified time. There are always neighborhood club meetings, environmental group meetings, Salvation Army suppers, or Rotary Club dinners after work hours. At least David had the good sense to know that he was not expected to go to all of them with me. If there was something involving labor or unions, people he knew, he would come with me. Otherwise, it was my deal.

Another vital part of being an officeholder is being on good terms with your workers. People will do their jobs much better and more happily if they feel they are being recognized for their work.

Very shortly after I was elected I had lunch with James Weir, the foreman of the Precinct Three road crew. James really had no interest in working for me; he was close friends with the man I had just defeated. I found him to be a reasonable and nice person, and by the end of lunch I told him that I would like him to stay on. He agreed to try it.

The next step was to meet the men.

The road office is the base for the men who actually

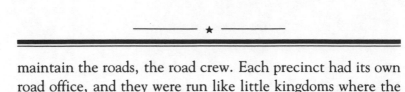

maintain the roads, the road crew. Each precinct had its own road office, and they were run like little kingdoms where the commissioner reigns. Johnny Voudouris had ruled this one for twelve years and the men were his. Some of them were highly skilled, others were not. They had worked very hard for his reelection; they knew how to get along.

These men had been told that they were all going to be fired and replaced by minorities and women, neither of whom they had much use for. Particularly women. They just did not want to go down to the beer hall on the weekend and have to say that their boss was a woman.

The road office was in a community called Oak Hill. It makes sense to put your road office near the roads—that way you don't have to move your equipment far. It was a grim and rainy day when we drove out, the kind where you really have to drag yourself out of bed. We pulled into the yard, and as I was about to climb the stairs to the heated loft where the meeting room and coffee pot were, I passed a dog. It was a real ugly, coarse-haired animal with big liver spots, and it was lying in the doorway all wet.

"My," I remarked as I started up the steps, "isn't that the ugliest old dog you've ever seen in your life?"

Upstairs there were about thirty men sitting on folding chairs and they had been gathered especially to hear me. I was their boss now and not only didn't they like it, there was nothing they could do about it. There was a real chasm between us.

But I needed these men. They knew where the roads were. I had some vague notion of the road system, but that was about it. If these men lay down on the job I was in big trouble.

I had prepared a speech about us all working together, and how important they were to me and to Precinct Three, and when I was finished I asked if they had any questions. Well, they all just sat there and stared at me and didn't say a word. This was not working out.

Finally, just to break the ice and get them talking, I asked them about their dog. Texas men will always talk about their dogs.

Nothing. No one said a word. There was some shuffling of feet.

I thought, "There must be something unseemly about the dog's name, it's the only answer." I looked around the room and they were ducking my gaze. "Let me tell you," I said, "that I am the only child of a very rough-talking father. So don't be embarrassed about your language. I've either heard it or I can top it.

"So, what's the dog's name?"

An old hand in the back row with a big wide belt and a big wide belt buckle sat up and said in a gravel bass, "Well, you're gonna find out sooner or later." He looked right at me. "Her name is Ann Richards."

I laughed. And when I laughed they roared. And a little guy in the front row who was a lot younger and a lot smarter than most, said in a wonderfully hopeful tenor, "But we call her Miss Ann!"

From then on those guys and I were good friends.

James Weir and I spent hours in his pickup and I quickly found out where the roads were. There really were little fiefdoms out there, each precinct with its own budget, its own equipment, its own suppliers. It was not the most efficient operation. Road and bridge money got tougher to come by each year, and at one point I tried to get the court to agree to a unitary road system, which would have benefited the county but altered the commissioners' power.

———— ★ ————

Under the system in place when I was elected, there were four separate road offices. Under a unitary road system we would pool our resources. We could run individual crews if we wanted, but rather than duplicating very expensive equipment we could cut the machinery budget and share the savings. Some machines were sitting idle half the time, and if we scheduled them through a central office we could put them all to use and save a ton of money.

I didn't have the staff or near enough money to commission the kind of technical study that would be necessary in order to sell this idea to the court, and I didn't feel right about asking the court to hire an engineering consultant. But I knew that we had to have some concrete data before I could bring the idea to the court's attention. So I called over to the University of Texas School of Business and found a young man named Tom Granger who agreed to do the study as a course project. I used his data to go before the court.

I was not successful in convincing the other commissioners to give up some of their power. But several years later they did institute a unitary road system and I believe there are substantial economies and savings being made there now.

There was a big loop being built around the western part of Travis County, and there was going to be a bridge built over the Colorado River. One of the issues in my campaign had been the rocks and boulders cascading down into the river at the bridge site, and the blight it caused on the landscape. My campaign literature had shown a photograph of the demolition, with earth and rubble spilling into the water.

I didn't want them to slap up one of those shortest-distance-between-two-points bridge monstrosities; this was one of the prettiest parts of the river and it shouldn't be despoiled. But, of course, when I went out to the Highway Department to review the design, it was everything I had feared it would be.

166

Just a straight, flat bridge with metal railings and stanchions plunging down into the water, anchored in huge cement protectors. Awkward industrial lights. It was just awful.

I contacted two architects, Hal Box and Chartier Newton. We were fools rushing in where angels fear to tread. They put together a slide show of beautiful bridges and accompanied me to a meeting with the Highway Department engineers.

So we were making our presentation and the engineers were sitting there, rolling their eyes, thinking, "Oh, Lord, deliver us from this," when one of them pulled me aside and said, "Ann, don't bring those architects back out here again; architects and engineers don't mix." I said, "I don't know any other way to get you all to take this bridge seriously. This is an opportunity for the Highway Department to really look good. I know if you put your heads to it you will come up with something that will make us proud."

They agreed that they would see what they could do. I said, "I'll keep in touch with you to see how you are doing."

They came up with a beautiful bridge. It is an arched span and the roadbed itself is supported by the structure. There are no stanchions into the water, and it's made of rusty Cor-Tin steel that blends in nicely with the hill country. I am really proud of that bridge.

Human services as well as roads fell under our jurisdiction, and when it came to human problems, by and large we had a sympathetic Commissioner's Court. For instance, we had an outstanding program of Travis County Services for the Deaf. There is a state-supported school for the deaf located in South Austin which consistently attracts many families of deaf children. People move into the area to send their children to the school, and then stay on and live in Austin.

Because the disability of deafness is not visible, it is hard to plead the cause of the deaf and get the money they need. Can you imagine what it is like to be deaf and be arrested, or try to go through a court proceeding? Just to involve yourself in routine commerce is a problem. You can't use a telephone unless you have a TTY machine which types out your messages as they are received; you don't know when the doorbell is ringing. I was involved in getting funding for programs for the deaf.

One of the other programs I was most proud of was called Infant Parent Training. It originated with federal funds and was developed for parents of Down's syndrome children.

It had been determined that with the right kind of parental guidance, Down's syndrome children could attend public school with other kids and lead relatively normal lives. But this training had to begin very early. In earlier times these children were discounted as vegetables, unfit for anything except institutionalization. Unnecessary institutionalization of any human being is a waste not only of human potential but of money; it costs a lot of money to maintain people in institutions, and the Infant Parent Training budget was about to be cut.

One of the frustrating things about dealing with people who have serious problems is that our instincts are to protect them, not to expose them publicly. It was felt for a long time in the social service field that you could best argue the case for people in need if the "professionals" did the talking. You didn't want to embarrass the people whom you were asking for money by confronting them with the clients to be served.

Well, once you remove the person in need from the decision-maker, the result is that the decision-maker is insulated from the real problem. You lose the passion.

I told the parents of the Down's syndrome children that I felt it was essential that they bring their children to the Commissioner's Court at budget time. There is a lot of difference between voting "No" with no one in the room and doing it when you see with your own eyes the people you are affecting.

Maybe twenty families came. You don't know how awesome it is to have the kind of responsibility we commissioners had over people's lives until you see a courtroom filled with Down's syndrome kids. We got the money.

I did the same thing with abused children. We thought the court was going to cut back on children's protective services, so I said, "Get me some photographs up here." When you see what happens to battered kids when there aren't enough funds to take them out of their environment, out of the house where they're being beaten, well, you can't sleep with that.

But on the whole, I felt that our entire approach to funding human services was wrong. As it stood, each agency that wanted or needed money had to prepare one budget for the Commissioner's Court, another for the city council, and a third for the United Way. Each governmental unit had a different fiscal year, so we would be pitted one against the other. It was a mess. We literally didn't know whether the clients were getting any real value; there was no way to monitor whether the agencies' human-services provisions were adequate, whether our dollars were being spent wisely.

We needed to form an approval body made up of the county, the city, the school district, and the United Way, to which all organizations would submit their budget requests. One organization, one budget, presented once a year.

Nothing in government happens really fast. That's the public's greatest protection, but it's also the greatest frustration. It took the city, county, state, and United Way a full year of meeting to agree to continue to meet. But finally we formed our approval board.

It's interesting that at that moment the human-services providers panicked. Either they didn't trust us or they were worried that their funds would be cut back. The net result was that the agencies began to talk among themselves for the first time and formed their own organization.

Because of my work in this area, Lieutenant Governor Bill Hobby appointed me to a committee to examine the delivery of human services in the state of Texas. At first I thought it was an honor, but it also turned out to be a tremendous amount of work.

On the committee with me were Frank Erwin, probably the most important single individual in the advancement of the University of Texas; Ted Strauss, a Dallas businessman whose wife, Annette, is now mayor of Dallas; Joachin Cigarroa of Laredo; Helen Farabee of Wichita Falls; Becky Canning of Waco; and June Hyer, the executive director. We found pretty much what you would expect; that it was a patchwork, that a number of people went unserved while other people were served doubly but not well.

My specific area of responsibility had to do with juveniles. The state of Texas had a county probation system which handled both juveniles and adults, but the adults were by and large the more serious offenders and the greater problems, so the juveniles were not getting sufficient attention and many of them were slipping through the cracks. We devised legislation that would offer state money for the formation of a probation system that would handle only juveniles, with the money released only if the individual counties matched it. This was strictly a carrot, not a bonanza. It was received very well, and as a result we created the state's first juvenile probation system.

I was very proud of that achievement. Most kids in trouble are there because they basically have little other choice. Either economic or social circumstances have made their future pretty bleak. Seventy-two percent of the juveniles who are serving time in the state of Texas have abused alcohol or drugs. Many of them have reading or learning disabilities. The answer society has devised is, "Let's lock them up and our problems will be solved." But you can't build enough buildings to lock them all up, you just can't. And once they are inside, we neither improve their life through education so that they are equipped once they get out of the lockup, nor counsel them adequately to help them deal with their addiction to alcohol or drugs. They are locked up with a bunch of kids exactly like themselves, so when they get back out on the street they have become far more sophisticated in criminal behavior.

And we shrug our shoulders and say, "Well, you know, that's the nature of it." And even more absurd is the fact that we are spending millions and millions of dollars at a time when money is getting harder and harder to come by, and spending it fruitlessly.

When I hear people saying on television and in the media that more kids are in trouble because of the breakdown of the family system, I really just want to climb the walls. Most women are working not because they choose to work but because they *have* to work. It makes better press and magazine copy to talk about career choices, and the wonderful opportunities for women. New opportunity is great—but that's not the real world for most women. Most women work at menial jobs, and they work because that is the only way they can support their families. They are not going to be in the kitchen with an apple pie when their kid comes home from school. And even if they were, if the kid is in pain from a learning disability, alcohol, or drugs, that pie won't be what he or she needs; counseling and help will be.

The Travis County Commissioner's Court worked to make it easier for people to register to vote. We set up substations at various places in the county where people could sign up, and lobbied to keep people from being purged from the voter rolls.

What a refreshing change! I used to sell poll tax. In Texas up until 1966, you had to buy the right to vote. We would set up card tables at grocery stores and try to get people to buy a poll tax. It's amazing to think how we got people to the polls at all in those days, when not only did they have to get there, they had to pay for the privilege.

With all these issues and answers, you might forget that government is really run by human beings, and the human comedy is very much at work. Strange things, goofy stuff, seemed to happen almost daily.

The Commissioner's Court was in charge of funding the county jail, and we had a continuing problem with the jail roof. The building was old and the roof had been patched so many times that a standing pool of water collected on it. No matter how many roofing experts we got up there to look at it or how many times the caretakers swept it out, they didn't seem to be able to drain that spot or stop the leaks.

One spring we had a terrible hailstorm. Hail the size of golf balls came winging out of the sky. As soon as the storm lifted, Richard Moya went running over to the jail to see what effect the hailstorm had had on the roof, and ran into Joe the repairman. Joe worked in the sheriff's office and helped out with menial jobs around the jail. Joe was distraught.

Richard came to my office and said, "You're not going to believe this. Joe is upset over that hailstorm. It killed his fish."

"Killed his fish?" I said.

"Killed his fish." Joe the repairman had gotten some goldfish and had chosen for their home that standing pool of water. Every day he would go up on the roof and feed them. Then the hailstorm came along and beat them to death.

Then there was the story of Doris and the pigeons.

Doris Shropshire, the county clerk, got a new car. When she parked it in the courthouse parking lot the pigeons who roosted on the jail ledges fouled it. Doris had read somewhere that rubber snakes would scare pigeons away, so she talked to Ralph, who was in charge of maintenance, and Ralph did a clean sweep of all the dime stores in Austin for rubber snakes.

So Ralph, doing as he was told, had to figure out how to get these snakes installed in the ornate masonry with which earlier generations of architects had thought to adorn the top floor of the courthouse where the jail was. No one told Ralph that if the system works at all, you have to coil these snakes and put them on the ledges. Pigeons are supposed to be scared of coiled snakes.

Ralph couldn't reach the crevices, so he tied his snakes to strings and attached them securely to the roof with lengths of rope.

The county commissioners didn't even know the snakes were up there. No one would have known if a pedestrian hadn't been passing by the jail one day and one of them fell on his shoulder and scared him almost to death.

It caused something of a stir. We all came out and looked up and, sure enough, blowing in the breeze, was a remarkable display of snakes.

The pigeons had been using them as a sanitation facility, fully covering the entire length with droppings until they became thick as baseball bats. It was not a pretty sight.

10

★

I DON'T believe I have talked sufficiently about women. During most of my lifetime women have been portrayed, and I think with some truth, as competing against each other for men's attention. The rule of thumb has been that if a woman was successful, in business or in any other field that had formerly been occupied by men, she became a queen bee who didn't remember, or didn't choose to help, those women who were still on a lower plane than she was. The competitiveness existed socially, and it certainly existed economically in the workplace.

In some ways, women have been their own worst enemies, partly because of the isolation of the lives we have led, and partly because that was what we thought we were supposed to be. But recently this has begun to change, and I have tried to do what I could to participate in this change.

I was working for Sarah Weddington when the United Nations passed a resolution proclaiming 1975 International Women's Year. Bella Abzug, serving in the U.S. House of Representatives at the time, introduced a bill the same year proposing a National Women's Conference as part of the Bicentennial celebration. President Gerald Ford ordered the creation of the National Commission on the Observance of

International Women's Year, "to promote equality between men and women," and directed it to deal "with those inequities that still linger as barriers to the full participation of women in our Nation's life."

By 1977 the inequities were still lingering and 20,000 women gathered in Houston to attend the National Women's Conference.

Hotels were jam-packed. Lady Bird Johnson was there with her daughter Lynda. Betty Ford, Rosalynn Carter, and Coretta Scott King were all on the platform. It was an exciting time because here was an opportunity for us to talk about the very serious problems affecting women. Our mandate was to come to a consensus on a statement of principles for the United States Government on the needs of women.

Barbara Jordan, congresswoman from Houston, was the Keynote speaker. She got a roar when she said, "Human rights apply equally to Soviet dissidents, Chilean peasants, and *American women*. Women are human. We know our rights are limited. We know our rights are violated. We need a domestic human rights program.

"This Conference could be the beginning of such an effort, an effort which would be enhanced if we would not allow ourselves to be brainwashed by people who predict chaos and failure for us.

"Tell them they lie—and move on."

Jimmy Carter had replaced Gerald Ford as president and had appointed Bella Abzug as presiding officer of this conference. Bella called and invited me over to her hotel to visit with her. I must admit I went, not with fear, but with some awe about meeting this woman who was so vociferous and outspoken.

She called me "Texas." "Texas," she said, "you've got some spunk." We were two entirely different people, from entirely different backgrounds, and I was pleased that there was a person of her stature who was speaking out strongly.

The conference was held at the height of the debate over the Equal Rights Amendment, and when the time came for the introduction of the ERA plank to the convention, we lined up at the microphones to be heard. Bella looked down and saw me and chose me to speak.

And so it was that I had the honor of making the first speech for the Equal Rights Amendment at the National Women's Conference. I spoke on behalf of "those few of us who are fortunate enough to be in the positions we are in, but also for those who are voiceless, the divorced woman who may not get credit, the widows who are incapable of making a living . . . my own daughter who cannot find women in the elementary school history texts of this country, and the men who encourage us and support equal rights."

It was tremendously exhilarating. The overriding sense of the conference was that, while we were going to disagree and disagree strongly, women realized that supporting each other was the hope of all our salvation. It was the beginning of saying that we women want to be friends with each other. It was extraordinary.

And it went beyond just being friends. Women had been friends back in my mother's living room, at the Home Demonstration Club, but they had been friends as an adjunct to other activities, secondary to things like cooking and cleaning and minding their husbands and children. This new vision of friendship was one in which it was all right to say out loud that we cared about the lives of other women.

This new friendship was not secondary to anything. We were saying that our lives would be improved and enriched by a support system, by talking out loud and helping to solve the needs of older women, who are the poorest of the poor; the problems of the single-parent woman raising children; the awful problems of poor and disadvantaged children themselves; the double stigma and difficulties of minority women. This was International Women's Year; we were saying that these problems were universal in the world.

It was a whole new way of thinking for women. Out of that fresh vision, and the scheduled meetings and activities, we learned some real-world skills and established relationships in which there was intrinsic trust. You could ask for help when you felt your own skills were lacking, and you would offer aid when asked.

Because of this conference I made contacts all over the country and I was often invited to other events. In the fall of 1978 the National Women's Educational Fund, sponsored by the Atlantic Richfield Corporation, held a conference in Aspen, Colorado, for women elected public officials. It was terrific to be around people who were facing the same kinds of problems I was.

The hue and cry among a lot of the women at the Aspen conference was "They won't take me seriously." And I do think that women have to work harder to gain respect. A lot of men are respected for who they are or what they have done, but women, regardless of who they are or what they have done, have to prove themselves over and over again.

The value in Aspen wasn't so much what we learned in the formal sessions as just being able to sit around and talk informally. The object of the conference was to discover what our commonalities were, and we found that, even in politics, there were issues that were set aside for us and others that were off limits. If it's legislation having to do with children or the disadvantaged or schools, that's women's work. The economy, diplomacy, defense, that's for the menfolk and we were not encouraged to take part.

Along about this time the National Women's Political Caucus was becoming more activist, with the goal of getting more women involved in politics and running for public office. We contributed to that effort by taking some of the game plan we used in my commissioner's race and adapting it for any race. Mary Beth Rogers had created a slide show for the National Women's Educational Fund that distilled what seems to be a complex activity into something very easy to understand.

Out of that slide presentation Jane Hickie and Mary Beth and I developed a kind of road show. We would travel all over Texas talking to political caucus groups, community groups, anyone who wanted to hear us, about how to get where they wanted to go.

But it quickly became obvious to us that there were a great number of women who didn't want to run for public office, who weren't particularly interested in politics, but who did want to learn the skills of how to get things done. These women didn't realize the real talents they had, they needed reassurance and confidence.

What evolved was that Jane, Mary Beth, and I would talk to any group that contacted us—the PTA, garden clubs, country-club ladies—and we would give How-To seminars, guidelines on how to be successful in PTA, community groups or before a city council. We were a new generation of Home Demonstration Ladies, but with a much wider menu!

These Texas women wanted to learn how to raise money, or how to approach someone who might not be interested in their cause. We talked about such simple things as body language, how crossed arms in front of your chest is a message of defiance, no matter what your words are saying; how people who sit back in their chairs convey the impression of being in command. They didn't know that if you wear a bunch of jangling jewelry or dangling earrings, people will be distracted from what you are saying.

Most of the women we talked to didn't know that when you make an approach to someone it should be in direct and simple language, not all of this, "Gee whiz, Bob, I wanted to talk to you about this last week but I didn't have a chance because the kids got sick and I had to go home early, and then you were gone on the trip and . . ." By the time you go through all that, the guy doesn't want to talk to you about anything.

I got more arcane in my discussions with the political women. I talked with them about color and how to use a microphone and television camera. We form quick and decisive judgments about the people we see on television, I said, and whether or not we want to listen to them is based on a lot more than words. Some colors translate well on the tube and some don't. With the advent of new cameras, reds, for example, do not do very well; there is an aura that comes off the image of red that is distracting. Busy prints on blouses or dresses also make a muddy and distracting picture.

There are certain colors, though, that look better on television. All the pastels are preferable to colors that are too brilliant. I remembered at the National Women's Conference, all the wives of presidents had on solid-color pastel outfits. When you're seen at a distance, on a stage or in a TV long shot, if people are going to remember you it's best to give them a clear target.

The television camera can read you like a book. You are liable to be asked anything, and the camera is grinding all the time and will register every nuance of expression. Any woman thinking of going into politics will have to learn to handle it. I suggested that while a woman is being interviewed she think of a person, preferably someone she really likes; her eyes will have a lot more warmth and sincerity if she's talking to a friend than to a machine. I often think of my daughter Ellen when I do interviews.

The key to doing an interview is to do it with the viewer in mind; not the interviewer, not the cameraman, not the camera. And watch yourself. Ask, "What are those people going to hear?"

There is also a lot of caution that must go into a television interview, because, in the age of the sound bite, a station or network is not going to use everything you say and their edits may distort completely what your conversation was really about. They know who their audience is; you must know yours.

Smiling on television is terribly important. When you sit and watch the television set at home, if the person on the screen smiles at you, you will in turn—in your living room—smile back at them. It's involuntary. You could say, "I have just run over your dog with a Mack truck," and smile while you are saying it, and the people in the living room will smile back.

Frowning is the same way. If you frown, you produce a sense of anxiety in the viewer.

Most people think they are supposed to be born knowing what to do with that television camera, but they aren't; it's a learned skill. Two friends of mine from Austin created a marvelous course called Thinking on Your Feet, which put women through the rigors of being interviewed with a microphone in their face and taught them direct language skills. I once filled in when one of them was pregnant, worked a convention, and had a wonderful time.

These workshops, both the overtly political and the generally social, were tremendously gratifying to me. In almost all cases, the women who attended left feeling better about themselves. And Jane, Mary Beth, and I did it for the joy of it. Because it was fun, and because it moved women along.

Sometimes the women wanted to talk about very personal problems. Sometimes all they knew was that they wanted to talk. I got a call inviting me to come to Llano, Texas, and speak about "women." Well, I thought the whole thing was sort of strange and peculiar, and I don't know what they thought I was—whether they believed we females who were involved in the cause of advancing women burned our bras and marched around in army boots—but I showed up. When I met this group they didn't know what to say. They needed someone to tell them it was okay just to be there. A great number of the women who came admitted that they had lied to their husbands about where they were going that night. I think they thought of us as a secret society, when in fact we were trying to be very public.

If you had asked me why I was doing this I would have told you that it was for Cecile and Ellen. I did not want two of my children to be denied advantages that were being given to my other two children. I had seen the difference in the amount of money that was spent in the public school system for my girls as opposed to my boys, and I would not abide it.

But at some point I had to look myself square in the mirror and say, "You are not doing this just for those girls, you are doing this for yourself too." It was a difficult realization and came as a big surprise.

All my life I had felt that one's motives had to be altruistic, that it was not okay to do things for yourself. Once you accept the fact that you are pursuing activity because it gives you some satisfaction and means something to you, then you have to accept responsibility for your actions, and then you have to accept responsibility for yourself. I wasn't used to doing that.

My first glimmerings of real independence were in serving on the Commissioner's Court. I was making decisions affecting people's lives, spending people's tax money, and I was making these decisions without asking David what to do. This was no small thing.

Most of my life I had led vicariously through someone else, seeing the world through someone else's eyes. I was used to speaking out, but in truth I relied on deferring to David. But the more I looked around, the more I found I was not alone in my predicament.

Some years before, I had read a news story about a woman

named Angelina Alioto, whose husband, Joseph Alioto, ran for governor of California. Both of them were probably in their fifties, and in the middle of the campaign Angelina Alioto ran away from home. Now, here was this lovely gray-haired patrician-looking woman in the middle of her husband's campaign, and she just took off. Disappeared. And she stayed gone for quite a while, a week or ten days.

It caused a sensation. Everyone said that it would be the end of her husband's political career, that he would be defeated. "What an embarrassment." But when she came back, and the press asked her why in the world she would do something like that, she said in essence that it was just assumed that her husband's running for governor was something that she wanted to do. She said they really had never talked about it, and that it had triggered something inside her. She realized that all her life she had been a good daughter to her parents, a good mother to her children, a good grandmother to her grandchildren, a good wife to her husband. But, she said, "I have never been me."

All of a sudden I was *being* me, and I was having a hard time handling it. Here I was spending all of my days in a public office and at night I was around all of my old political friends, and after-hours there was always political talk at the parties and at the table. And my friends would discuss events and would come to totally erroneous conclusions or have the facts wrong. And I would know they were wrong because I had been in the room when the events had happened!

Can you imagine the difference? For all these years I had listened to this talk and I had taken it as gospel truth, but of course what I had heard was whatever spin whoever was talking had put on it. Now suddenly I was in a position where I *knew* they were wrong.

Well, what do you do? Do you say, "You're crazy as a bedbug, that's not what happened"?

What a threat to our little circle. Politics was no longer in the realm of theory and fantasy and philosophy; there was an ugly note of reality injected into it. And I was the one who injected it. All of a sudden I was an authority.

I know that it had an effect on the dynamic of my relationship with David. I don't know whether he realized it, but I sure did. Sometimes when he had something particularly in error I would confront him, but most times I did not. Often I had been in meetings where confidences had been exchanged and I couldn't reveal them, and I didn't. Sometimes I would just listen and let it go.

I had been so admiring of David because of how much he knew; the richness of his schooling and his background was far beyond anything that I would ever know. I could have started studying that day and would never have caught up to him. David was so bright and quick. And here all of a sudden there were situations in which he was dead wrong. I was stunned.

We had traveled along the same road for twenty-some-odd years and then suddenly my life just went straight up like a skyrocket. New experiences, new people, new ideas, new activities, and David was still doing the same thing he had always done. He was very good at it, but it was hard on him and a terror on me. I started thinking about it all the time, and what I saw happening was that my most valued relationship was beginning to spin out of my control. And the harder I reached for it, the more elusive it became.

The marriage felt like a top that was spinning away from me and I could not get it back.

It couldn't have been easy for David, either. There are lots of women of my generation whose lives have changed dramatically, but not so many men. If the men of my father's generation went to school, they started a career and a profession, and then World War II came along. They left their jobs, went to a new place, learned a new job, and came home after the war. Everyone applauded and welcomed them back. They had a total break in the routine of their lives, and they picked up their old jobs with renewed enthusiasm.

Most of the men in my generation didn't have that break. They got out of school, entered a profession, and stayed there. End of story. Now here I was making my way in the world and I felt the unity of our relationship beginning to come apart.

It was devastating, and there didn't seem to be anything I could do about it. Usually I could think my way to a clear course of action, but there was so much craziness going on within me that there really was nothing that I could do. There was a sort of wall; I couldn't figure out who I was. I was staggering beneath the stresses of being the perfect wife, the perfect mother, the perfect hostess, and this new public persona with all of the weight one feels from serving in public office and working very hard to make all the perfect decisions.

And the phone kept ringing.

David and I had a game we played. The phone would ring and he would answer it, and if it was for me he would cup his hand over the receiver, point it toward me, and say, "Ann, it's King Kong," or "Ann, it's the governor." Someone I didn't want to talk to. Usually it was Virginia Whitten on the line.

So the phone rang one Sunday and David answered it, cupped his hand over the receiver, and said, "Ann, it's Midge Costanza."

I swept up the phone and said very cavalierly, "Hi, Midge, what do you want? I'm cooking David's supper."

There was a stunned pause on the other end of the line. "Uh, Ann, President Jimmy Carter has asked me to call you to see if you would be willing to serve on his Advisory Committee for Women."

Oh, I was so embarrassed. "My God, Midge . . ." I was

184

apologizing as fast as I could. "I had no idea it was really you. . . ." Midge Costanza was Jimmy Carter's special assistant, the highest-ranking woman in the administration, and I was talking to her like a cranky neighbor. "Of course I accept. I am honored to be considered and I'll be thrilled to serve."

The Advisory Committee meetings were held in Washington, D.C., and there were women of every conceivable interest and agenda on it: disabled women, Native American women, Pacific Asian-American women, black women, clubwomen, older women, Hispanic women (and by Hispanic women I mean Cuban-Americans, Puerto Rican-Americans, and women whose origins were Mexican), and some others as well. We did not all necessarily agree with each other. Everyone had her own particular issue, and coming to some consensus was going to be an onerous task.

Bella Abzug was the chair of this committee. We were funded through the Department of Labor, represented by a very able liaison named Alexis Herman, and our mandate was to advise the president what we felt needed to be done in terms of federal legislation or initiatives.

Foremost in our minds was the Equal Rights Amendment, which touched us all. We met several times to get things organized, divided ourselves into interest groups for study, and came back with recommendations.

I was sick with the flu when the Advisory Committee met with President Carter. The purpose of the meeting was to find out what he wanted from us and what we wanted from him.

From all reports, it was a disaster. Somehow President Carter got the impression that Bella intended to say something that would embarrass him publicly, perhaps accuse him of not fully supporting the ERA, I'm not sure. During or directly after the meeting Bella was called aside by Hamilton Jordan and told that she was no longer the chair of the committee.

More than half the committee resigned in protest. Midge Costanza resigned a short time later. I had not attended the meeting and as a consequence didn't really know that much about what had actually happened, but I got a couple of phone calls asking me to issue a public statement and resign as well.

Certainly the energy would be gone from the enterprise, and I didn't see how further involvement in it was going to be particularly productive. But Sarah Weddington had gone to Washington to work at the Department of Agriculture, and, lo and behold! she was hired to take Midge Costanza's place. I felt a great deal of loyalty to Sarah, so I stayed on to try and help.

Some women who also stayed were not happy. Their loyalties were to Midge and Bella, and they were not sure how they would fit in the new scheme of things. The entire effort was very, very difficult. New women were named to the committee and the business began again to try to get something accomplished.

The issue came up of who was going to succeed Bella as chair. I felt we needed someone who would have some credibility, some clout, someone who was not necessarily a part of the women's movement as such and who would really give us an opportunity to get things done. We came up with the name of Lynda Johnson Robb. She was Lyndon's daughter, and her husband, Chuck, was running for lieutenant governor of Virginia. Lynda agreed to serve, and served ably. She brought in people who had been in the Johnson administration and who understood the workings of Washington, and they were very good.

The mission of the second committee was not as diverse as the first. We felt strongly that if this committee could do one thing it would be to focus on those states which had not yet ratified the Equal Rights Amendment, to try and turn them to our side. To that end we brought women from those wavering states to Washington and asked them what their problems were in getting the ERA passed, and what we could do to help.

The meeting was held at Blair House. I remember Missouri being there, and Louisiana, Illinois, probably Florida. The women talked to various members of the committee, and immediately after these discussions we went across the street to the White House.

We had been led to believe that Jimmy Carter personally was willing to help the cause, and we had what we felt was a pretty good list of things the president could do to get the Equal Rights Amendment passed. Things like contacting members of the business community in Georgia, for instance the president of Coca-Cola, and saying, "This item is a matter of seriousness; is there any way you might be able to help?" There was a major highway project in Illinois and some pending laws concerning the shoals off the Carolina coast, both of which might be used in some sort of political leverage, but in truth none of us thought that the president really was going to hold up legislation on behalf of the ERA.

We went into the White House and sat down in a great big long room with a great big long conference table, and it was agreed that Lynda would open the remarks with the president and then I would present the overall concept of our proposals.

The president entered. The night before, when we all had been invited to dinner in the White House family quarters, he had come in wearing his jeans and a shirt. Mrs. Carter is a strong woman and had strong feelings about the advancement of women, and she and the president had been very gracious. This time, he was all business.

Mrs. Carter attended the meeting too. Lynda Robb said, "Mr. President, we are grateful to you for giving us this opportunity to speak with you. The needs of women are diverse and we are grateful for your personal involvement." Then she turned to me and said that I was going to give him the gist of

187

the meetings we had just held at Blair House, and the sense of our commission.

I again thanked the president for the opportunity to be there and to present our recommendations. I said, "Mr. President, it is our impression that you are willing to personally make some calls on behalf of our interests, and of central interest to all of us is the passage of the Equal Rights Amendment. We feel that there are areas and people that you might contact who would be helpful in the individual states." I was about to continue when the president interrupted.

"Frankly, ladies," he said sternly, "I am *very* disappointed."

Well, none of us knew what to say. The president went on to tell us that he thought we were going to come back and tell him what *we* intended to do to pass the ERA. He did not expect *us* to be a group that would come in, like everyone else did, and tell him the things that *he* needed to do.

What was there left to say? Several people spoke briefly, but I can't remember what they said. We were all just stunned. We thanked him, and as we went out we all got our pictures made.

Lynda Robb did not want to meet with the press. The White House Press Room would test the mettle of the heartiest of souls, so Lynda said to me, "You have to go talk to the press."

I went in there and, surprisingly, I was not afraid of them. I was going to put the very best spin on it I possibly could. I said we had met with the president, that we had had an exchange of ideas, and that the president was supportive of our efforts. It was exactly like you see it on TV. Sam Donaldson shouted at me, "Well, what's he gonna do?!" And I answered that we didn't have the specifics ironed out yet. Helen Thomas wanted to know if Jimmy Carter really was for the Equal Rights Amendment. I said that, certainly, indeed he was.

I finished that bath of fire and went over to the Hay Adams

with my two best friends on the commission, Ann Ramsey and Erma Bombeck. We sat down and I said, "Well, boy, you know, I can't get over that. That was totally unexpected." Erma was not quite so stunned. She had been on the original commission and had gone to that fateful meeting where Bella had been dismissed. She said, "You know, the interesting thing to me was that that's the same thing he said the last time we went to the White House."

The Equal Rights Amendment was a real problem for the Carter administration. It was a political hot potato. The heat really got turned up by the right wing, and in retrospect I see that we were naive in thinking that we might get it adopted. The states that passed the ERA—in Texas it passed in 1972 as part of the state constitution at the same time that we ratified it for the national constitution—didn't really have that much difficulty, because it is an innocuous amendment.

But in the mid-seventies, the right wing of this country was in disarray. Spiro Agnew had been driven out of office, Nixon had been driven out of office, and there was nothing to fuel the fire of the tract mailings that went into the rural mailboxes. The Equal Rights Amendment was used as a vehicle to keep their troops organized.

That's when all of the absurd claims involving sexual mixing got into it: the business of boys and girls being forced to use the same bathroom—which was so ridiculous. I mean, boys and girls use the same bathroom at home. They use the same bathroom on airplanes. All of a sudden girls were going to be required to get into foxholes with men. The right wing got organized and they did a good job, and they built a level of fear that ultimately made the ERA impossible to ratify.

David and I were always trying to instill in our children a love of Texas. At some point the whole family went down to San Antonio to visit the Texas Institute of Cultures, an enormous

building that housed a tremendous collection of Texana artifacts and pictorial displays. We sat in the large central rotunda and watched an exciting, stirring slide show projected on the concave ceiling. It was truly thrilling and gave me a real sense of pride in my state.

When it was over and we were lining up to walk through the exhibits, Ellen, who couldn't have been more than seven or eight years old, tugged at my sleeve and said, "Where were all the women?"

I had missed it. The program had been a pictorial display of Texas history, and everybody knows that history is pretty much the story of men. Our history is a story of wars. There had been a couple of women in the slide show: Lillie Langtry, who was English, not a Texan at all; and Elizabeth Ney, an avant-garde sculptor. But that was it.

When I got home I really began to wrestle with the question. How were little girls like my daughters going to come up with any understanding of who they are or where they'd come from, if they had no history? I knew that my sons, in watching that show, must have felt very proud, but my daughters would certainly not come away with any sense of themselves as Texans.

I was already a member of the board of the Texas Foundation for Women's Resources, whose board of directors consisted of Cathy Bonner, Martha Smiley, Jane Hickie, Judith Guthrie, Sarah Weddington, and me. Among the work we had already done was write and produce a book called *Women in Public Office*, which told stories about the contributions of women whom students would probably not otherwise get to read about.

In most cases the women that had been elected in Texas were elected because their husbands had died in office, or, as in the case of "Ma" Ferguson, had been impeached. Ma Ferguson—known by that name because her husband, the governor, was called "Pa" Ferguson—was elected governor twice following Pa's downfall. My favorite story about her involved punishing children for speaking Spanish in the public schools. Ma said, "If the English language was good enough for Jesus Christ it's good enough for the schoolchildren of Texas."

So I came home and was wrestling with the whole idea that there is no history of women in Texas and that we should do something to correct it. I got the board to agree that the project was worthwhile and that if I would do the legwork they would be happy to help.

I went over and talked to Mary Beth Rogers, who was running her own public relations firm at the time and had the discipline, marketing technique, and writing ability to get a project like this accomplished. I told her, "Mary Beth, this is not going to be any big deal. All you'll have to do is to deal with the people down at the Institute of Texan Cultures—and we will help you do that."

Four years and $400,000 later the exhibit opened.

It was a monumental task. It turned out that there was no history. We couldn't put an exhibit together because we didn't have any information, there weren't any materials. We had a source here and there, but the most notable Texas woman was the woman in the Alamo who'd had sense enough to leave before she got herself killed. We had to survey all Texas libraries, museums, university history departments, anything we could think of that might have information about the state's women.

Thousands of survey sheets came back and we learned things about Texas women, individually and in groups, that most of us had never known.

Catherine Stinson, one of the first women in America to fly, made her first solo airplane flight in 1912, eleven years before Charles Lindbergh started his flight training. She set endurance and distance records, did sky writing, flew loop-the-loops, tried to enlist in the Air Corps in World War I but was turned down because she was female, and then flew airmail service for the government.

Native American women of Texas, who were basically the architects of their tribes, were the people who designed the tepees; ingenious designs for structures that must be easily collapsed, moved, reassembled, and accommodate varying temperatures.

Black women, who were involved with church activities and were closely involved with the needs of their children, had a strong history. A woman named Jeffie O. A. Conner, a Home Demonstration agent in McLennan County in 1925, convinced the school district to make drinking cups out of tin cans so that each child had his or her own rather than sharing a common dipper which had been spreading disease. Black laundresses in Galveston called the first strike of organized labor in Texas; they had been working for something like a nickel a day. Twelve thousand San Antonio pecan shellers, who had been making less than three dollars for a fifty-four-hour week, went out on a long, bitter, famous strike in 1938 led by a Hispanic woman named Emma Tennayuca. She was about nineteen years old at the time.

There were women rodeo riders, women involved in establishing museums, women doctors, lawyers, scientists, educators. The motto of the Waco Women's Club was "If we rest, we rust."

Women were the civilizers of Texas. There's a good story about the T. L. K. Temple lumber company in Diboll, out in East Texas, that was having a hard time hanging on to employees. The men's work was sporadic, they'd work three days and then get drunk for three days; it was a brawling atmosphere. Finally, in 1894, the company advertised in an Eastern newspaper for a woman—one woman—to come and set up a "society" in Lufkin. Not high society, just a community life. And Fannie Farrington came and started a school and a church and began to make the place suitable for families to live, with the end result that the lumber company had a stable work force.

There was a woman named Clara Driscoll who was smart and good-looking and had a lot of money, and before she was twenty-three years old she wrote the checks that saved the Alamo from being demolished. Her father was a South Texas rancher and a millionaire, and she was an author and a playwright and a politician and a diplomat. One of the stories I love the most about her was that she contributed $30,000 to one of Franklin Delano Roosevelt's campaigns—an extremely significant amount of money in those days—and after he was elected, Roosevelt named her husband ambassador to Chile. Not her, her husband. So much for good works.

The treasures we discovered were rich, but no one had ever pulled them together before. Mary Beth and the staff drove around the state looking at the artifacts that were available to us. Most things were only available on loan and for a short period of time; they were family treasures and had to be returned. We got the Mixmaster used by Betty Graham when she made the first formula for Liquid Paper, the typewriter white-out. We obtained a pair of boots made by Enid Justin, president of Justin Boots, and the HK branding iron of Henrietta King of the King Ranch.

We knew that because most women would not be able to come to San Antonio to see the exhibit, the history project would be seen by a limited number of people. So what started as an archive became a traveling exhibit. Chula Reynolds helped raise money to establish both the exhibit and the traveling show, and she became a member of the board. With the help of various grants, a portable project was designed that could be erected in shopping malls and bank lobbies, places where people could see it.

A wonderful side benefit of this exhibit was that for the first time there was a serious cataloguing of women's material, and it offered an opportunity for the media to write about women in Texas history. The exhibit became a prototype for other states, and both Virginia and Colorado have since created similar exhibits. The Texas collection and archives is at Texas Woman's University.

I never like to say that there is something about Texans that sets us apart; I do feel that people across the country are unified by being Americans. But every state does have its identity, and if there is something different about us it is that Texas was a frontier, and the people who came here had to be adventurous and hardworking to survive, and I think that spirit remains and is passed on.

Unfortunately, most of the stories that people read about the identity of Texas are very much about maleness, about cowboys slumped in their saddles. But that's because most of the people who wrote the books were men. I understand that; you write about what you know. Celia Morris had a wonderful phrase. She said, "The history of Texas is pretty much the history of what men do outdoors."

But whatever is in that hardy frontier spirit is in the women as well as the men. Some of the stories we unearthed would break your heart. The women were left with the responsibility of running ranches and households while the men went off and fought the wars or drove cattle. A lot of these women lived in sod huts, dugouts. Water was always scarce, and there was so much sickness and loneliness. There was no church or school or people to talk to. Some of them had to ride for days to even see another human being.

There was a story about a ranch woman named Maryann Goodnight. From time to time cowboys would stop by and she would give them a meal. One day a cowboy rode into camp with three chickens in a sack, and instead of killing, plucking, and cooking them, she kept them for pets. She said no one could ever know how much company they were.

One artifact that we found was called a "crazy jug." Around 1886 a woman named Lizzie Campbell lost a child, and she had no one living nearby, no friends or relatives to share her grief. So to keep her baby's memory with her, she took a little bottle and glued keepsakes and her child's mementos to it, and the bottle has been handed down now for a hundred years.

My favorite piece in the exhibit was a crazy quilt, simple but beautiful patterns, sometimes with a prize piece of cloth but mostly just odds and ends. Along with the quilt was a quotation from a book called *The Quilters* with which I felt a real affinity:

> *Sometimes you don't have no control*
> *over the way things go.*
>
> *Hail ruins the crops or fire burns you out.*
>
> *And then you're just given so much*
> *to work with in a life and you have to do*
> *the best you can with what you got.*
>
> *That's what piecing is.*
>
> *The materials is passed on to you*
> *or is all you can afford to buy . . .*
> *Your fate.*
>
> *But the way you put them together*
> *is your business.*
> *You can put them*
> *in any order you like.*

11

★

IN the late seventies we had a lot of friends in Austin who had moved here from other parts of the state. I didn't want them to just live here—I wanted them to love living here. I wanted them to feel about Texas the passion that I feel.

Texas is the most diverse of states. The only thing we don't have is year-round snow-capped mountain peaks. We've got just about everything else. The Texas you see in magazines is a vast, empty stretch of flatland that goes on forever, and we do have an awful lot of Texas that is like that: mostly West Texas and the Panhandle. Of course, under that flatland is lots of oil, and in its own way that's very beautiful. In West Texas the sky wraps around you like a blanket. The Palo Dura Canyon out near Amarillo is simply spectacular; Georgia O'Keeffe spent some time teaching school and painting there. The Piney Woods of East Texas are vast and gorgeous forests of conifers. The black lands of Central Texas around Waco where I grew up have a lot of river bottoms with pecans growing alongside the rivers. South Texas has a moderate climate and there are citrus groves and some of the most beautiful beaches in the country. It has the fishing industry and a sort of laid-back ambiance not unlike Mexico. The Big Bend country, where the Rio Grande divides Mexico from Texas has awe-inspiring canyons and mountains. I don't know of any other state that has all of that, plus very cosmopolitan cities, and cities with the romantic flavor of San Antonio.

I wanted my friends to know the state with the same intensity I did, so I started a little project called Know Your Texas.

I would, from time to time, plan weekend camp-outs. With David's suggestions, we would travel all over the state and act as tour guide and social director for whoever wanted to come along. We would all take our tents, or rent cabins if we were in a state park. Sometimes our caravan was as small as two other couples, mostly it was about thirty people, kids and all, out for adventure.

We would try to impart as much information as we could. I would mail out directions and instructions: now is the time, here's where we're going, here's what you ought to know about it.

We had a great time down near Uvalde, in Garner State Park, which is one of my favorite parks. The buildings and the furniture in the buildings were constructed by the Civilian Conservation Corps during the Roosevelt administration, and they're really quaint cabins with solid heavy handmade furniture. This park is on the Frio River, which is clear and beautiful and cold. Everyone would bring canoes; you might make a one-day run. There are big stands of cypress trees and a stretch of road that is really stunning.

We also went to South Padre Island, which at the time was just miles of untouched beaches and undeveloped land. We went to the Toledo Bend reservoir on the Louisiana-Texas border. We went all over.

We didn't necessarily travel trunk-tail, trunk-tail; there would be logistics to all of us hooking up at the right place and right time. Everyone would bring food and there would be a communal campfire. We would plan the meals together so that we all weren't cooking separately, but by and large everyone was equipped.

Every time we left on one of those things and David had to pack the car, there was lots of *hmmmmm*ing and grinding of teeth, because I always wanted to be sure that we had everything we needed. We not only had to have the food we were going to eat, but things for the kids to do, cards and games. We carried *The Handbook of Texas* with us in the car and we would read aloud from it as we went through places, and talk about where we were going and what had happened there.

I liked to camp out. David and I had been taking the kids on weekends, looking for a place where we could spend some time away from town, and we found a farm on the North San Gabriel River. We split the property with our friend John Huber and got the run of about 200 acres, a little white farmhouse, and access to the river front.

We did a lot of painting and cleaning and refurbishing, but it was still a teeny noninsulated house, blazing hot in the summer and freezing cold in the winter. So very quickly we opted to just camp out at the river. We cleared a kind of thicket and called it the Bosque Dell, pronounced "Bosky." I liked that phrase, Bosque Dell. I don't have any idea what it means. But in that thicket we had a natural windbreak, and about a half-dozen times a year or more we would have camp-outs there.

Any time we were setting up camp the word would get out and anywhere from two dozen to sixty people would come. Everyone would set up their tents around the outside, with the central cooking fire in the middle. It was a massive blaze, with a bountiful supply of firewood.

People would come from out of town to be there. The fire was ringed by a circle of ankle-high stones about twenty or thirty feet across, and everyone would sit around it. Wayne Oakes had his guitar, Stan Alexander would play and sing, Molly Ivins would spin tales, Mary Holman would get up and dance a jig around the fire. There would be a lot of storytelling and a lot of drinking late into the evenings. I certainly did more than my share of drinking.

We had a diverse group of friends, most of whom were ready for just about anything. At one point in the seventies, our friend Eddie Wilson called us and said that he had something wonderful that he wanted to show us. David and I went with him over to see a place that looked like an airplane hangar. It was just enormous—a great cavernous place. Most of the windows were up high and were broken out, and it was all cobwebby and had many years of filth and about a city block of junk stored in it. Eddie said, "Look at this wonderful place. This is going to be the biggest and best music spot in Texas."

Well, Eddie was always given to exaggeration, and David and I looked at each other and thought, "Lord help us, what is he off on now?" And that dirty barn became the Armadillo World Headquarters, and some of the biggest music acts in the country played there. Waylon Jennings, Willie Nelson, Bette Midler, the Pointer Sisters all appeared as well as any country and western group that you could think of. There was a very active and influential music scene in Austin in the seventies and the Armadillo was the lead dog, packing them in by the thousands on weekends. David and I loved the music and would go over there quite a lot to see Eddie and his partner, Mike Tolleson.

When the Armadillo got to be such a hit, Eddie started another place down on 3rd and Trinity called the Raw Deal. It was a hangout where you could get grilled chicken, basic but really good food. We used to go down there a lot. Eddie sold the

Raw Deal to another good friend of ours, Fletcher Boone. We would go down to visit Fletcher at the Raw Deal on Friday nights and eat supper and drink beer. Fletcher became so successful with the Raw Deal that he opened another one out on 6th Street.

Fletcher is a story in himself. He's an artist and a sculptor, and at one time he had an art gallery that was over at 600 West 28th Street. It so happened that, on the building, the 6 looked kind of like a G, and we called his place Gallery Goo. After we had been down to the Raw Deal on Friday nights, lots of times we would end up at the Gallery Goo.

Some of our running mates included Jap Cartwright and his wife Phyllis, and Bud Shrake and his wife Doatsy. Bud and Jap put together an organization called the Mad Dogs. They had calling cards printed that said Mad Dogs, Inc., with the motto, "Doing Indefinable Services for Mankind." They really were silly, funny, wonderful, mad.

The Mad Dogs were in Dallas one weekend and they decided that the decisive factor in determining their actions for the evenings was, "Would the King approve?" The King in question was Farouk. So the big question, no matter where they went, was, "Is this where the King would want to go?" Or, "Is this what the King would want to do?" It was posed and pondered loudly at every turn.

Jap and Phyllis had a Christmas party and we all went in costume. I went dressed as Dolly Parton one year, but this time I came as Santa Claus. David and I had left and come home at a halfway decent hour, and when I woke up the next morning I could tell it was still very early. I was mixing in what I was hearing with whatever my dream had been, and somehow I thought my father was coming downstairs to my bedroom.

My bedroom door burst open and in came Jap and Bud, plus Jerry Jeff Walker, all dressed in what they insisted on calling their Flying Punzar outfits. They were attended by their wives, whom they were referring to as their groupies.

The Punzars were Mad Dog inventions. They were a team of crazed acrobats given to impromptu exhibitions of derring-do. The Punzar costumes were long black tights, a black T-shirt with a lightning bolt slashing across the chest, and a little cape that hung maybe down as far as the waist. Now, Bud is about six feet six, and of course they just don't make tights for people that big, so he looked ridiculous. In fact, they all did.

They had been up all night and they had come to get Santa Claus.

David was already up making coffee, so it didn't take a lot of convincing to get us to go with them down to Bud's house.

Now, the goal of the Punzars was to Do the Triple. This was high gymnastics. Bud would stoop down, lace his fingers, cup his hands and put them between his knees. Jerry Jeff would position himself several feet away as the Catcher. Jap would come and put his foot in Bud's hands and Bud would give a big lift, and the goal was for Jap to turn a triple somersault in the air and for Jerry Jeff to catch him.

Well, of course the result was that they were falling into tables, knocking over furniture. Bud's wife Doatsy finally had enough of that.

I got a note from Bud before the Keynote speech saying that the Punzars stood ready to entertain either before or after my presentation, whichever was needed.

12

★

THINGS were not improving in our marriage.

David and I never fought, which was probably a failing rather than a blessing. We rarely had arguments, but the marriage was slipping beyond my grasp, and as it did I drank more and more. I don't want to suggest that that was the cause of my drinking. I only know that the pain of living was less with alcohol.

A lot of times in the afternoon, after work, I would go over to Nick Krajl's place, called the Quorum, and have drinks with Bob Bullock and Frank Erwin and whoever happened to be there. There were always lots of people sitting around drinking after work. It had gotten dark early one evening when I turned to Erwin and said, "I've got to go home and be a wife and mother." He looked at me and said, with laughing resignation, "You won't like it."

I went to a doctor and told him that I was worried about my drinking. He asked me, "How much do you drink?"

"I drink as many as three or four martinis a night," I told him.

"Oh, don't worry about that," he said, "I drink that much myself."

202

I didn't know a lot about alcoholism then. I know a great deal about it now. Most medical schools teach nothing about addiction, and a common thread in psychiatry is that if you get rid of the cause of the drinking you will then get rid of the drinking. Well, that's wrong. There can be a million causes, a million excuses, but basically alcoholism is a biological, physiological disease.

People who drink to excess, or use drugs to excess, think that everyone does. And they think that the effect that alcohol or drugs has on them is the effect it has on everyone else. One of the reasons they think that everyone is doing what they're doing is that, by and large, they run with people who do. And so alcohol becomes a way of life. What may start as an occasional drink or a beer progresses into a drink and wine with dinner, or a couple of drinks and wine with dinner, or a drink before going to a party where you already know there will be more drinking. With the alcoholic, the habit becomes a necessity.

The picture that practicing alcoholics have of alcoholics is the same that the general public has: that is, people who are asleep in doorways with bottles of cheap wine, or passed out under bridges, or causing automobile accidents. But there are thousands of alcoholics who aren't doing any of that, who are functioning very well in their own way. Many alcoholics are tough, resilient people who are out to prove that they can do more drunk than ten people can do sober.

In my own case I think that I was fortunate in that it was very hard for me to drink a lot and stay awake. I never got into the kind of drinking where you have a drink before you go to work in the morning. And that's another mistaken notion about alcoholics, that they drink all day long. I've known a lot of alcoholics who would stay drunk for three or four days and then not drink anything for three months, mainly to prove to themselves that they were not alcoholics. Binge drinkers. They would tell themselves, "Since I can go without it, then I'm not an alcoholic."

I would drink a lot after I got off work, and on weekends. I was screaming for someone to help me, rescue me. I don't know from what. From myself. I couldn't hear it but I was saying, "I'm so afraid and so desperate, and I can't keep up, and the only thing that really matters to me is falling apart."

My children mattered to me a lot, but I thought that I would die if I were not married to David Richards. And the relationship was simply beyond reclaiming. We had grown so far apart. I felt frightened, rejected. I desperately needed a way out but I didn't know what it was.

Jane Hickie watched my deterioration and was determined to do something about it. I don't know from what source, but she found a couple named John and Pat O'Neill in Austin who run programs that teach families how to intervene in the life of an alcoholic.

David was very reluctant to participate, so Jane asked my son Dan and Michael Sharlot to come with her and convince him. Together they got his approval, and then they all had to go to classes for several days to receive instruction in what they were to do. I, of course, didn't know any of this at the time.

Sunday morning, September 27, 1980, my good friend Sue Sharlot came over to my house. She said that her father had had an accident, or was sick, and that she was worried about it and would I come to her house and be with her. I said sure. I got dressed and drove over.

When I walked in her door, there were all my best friends sitting in a circle. There were Tony and Claire Korioth, Jane Hickie, Sam and Virginia Whitten, Sue and Michael Sharlot, Sarah and Standish Meacham, my children Cecile and Dan, David, and this couple, the O'Neills.

I was frightened. I thought something had happened to

one of my children. Clark was studying in Japan and Ellen was away at school. I said, "Are the children all right?" I was assured that they were.

Then the professionals, the O'Neills, took over. There was a chair and they said, "Won't you have a seat? Your friends want to tell you that they are concerned about you." And then each person in that circle read a prepared statement.

They were very specific. They didn't say things like, "You've acted like a jerk." They told me things about myself. I was in such a state of shock that I really don't remember much of what anyone said. Except for Tony Korioth. Tony said that one time I had been at a Fourth of July party at their house and Ann Korioth, who is my namesake and is their only daughter, had been sitting with me. I had held on to her hand and she had tried to get out of my lap, and I continued to hold on to her hand, and Tony thought that I had hurt her. I had certainly scared the little girl. And the last line of all of the statements was, "And I know you would not have done that if you had not been drinking."

They were trying to make me see a specific action and a direct relation to the alcohol.

I listened to each person in turn. It was overwhelming. Unbelievable. A trauma beyond any that you can imagine, and with a dozen people speaking for three or four minutes each, it went on for a while.

Feelings came and went. I was so terribly frightened. And then I felt a wash of relief that perhaps there was some way out for me. I felt anger, a lot of anger, at David and some of the others; I thought, "You're being pretty hypocritical, you were with me drinking all the way."

When the circle was over, Mr. O'Neill said, "We would like for you to seek treatment. There is help for this disease."

It was awful for them too, and I felt a lot of real pain for my friends, who were pressed to the point that they had to go

this far for me. I was sitting there crying and so were they.

So I asked where I could go that would give me the best shot at recovery, and the O'Neills told me there were a number of places but the best place was St. Mary's Hospital in Minneapolis, and that they had the plane tickets and that I was to leave around three o'clock that afternoon.

I went home and packed. I didn't want David to go with me, I was so angry and hurt with him, but finally he flew up there with me.

I was terrified. I thought that when I went into the hospital the world would be over for me. I was a public person, there was no way I could survive it.

St. Mary's was not a hospitable-looking place. It was an old building and there were no frills. The first night I was put in a room with a woman who was suicidal. I thought, "Oh, my God, I don't know that I can handle this."

I asked for and was granted a room by myself. Most hospitals will not allow you to do that, but I really think it was my salvation. I was so crushed and wounded and terrified that I needed a place to retreat, almost like bears hibernate in the winter or an injured animal finds a lair to repair itself.

I kept a diary for a while there. It's very hard for me to read now because it is so desperate. I was so worried about what people would think, because for a long time in my life what people thought of me mattered a great deal.

One thing I got over right away was any feeling of anger or animosity toward my friends. I realized how very hard that intervention had been for them, and how much they loved and cared for me for them to do that. To put themselves through that kind of pain for me was sort of an ultimate expression of friendship and I still feel a tremendous gratitude to them.

In the hospital each of us was assigned a counselor and we were all assigned to a group. Most of the work was done in group therapy. We had exercises to perform, and some of them were pretty interesting. We had to figure out the first time we had ever had anything with alcohol in it, and then we had to figure out how much we had drunk from that time to the present, and then we had to attach a dollar amount so that we could see, in dollars, how much it had cost us.

We had to make a list of all of the physical accidents that had occurred because we were impaired from drinking. Like the time I broke my leg; I knew it was directly related to having had too much to drink and then stepping on a doormat that went out from under me. (The accident and illness rates in this country that are directly attributable to alcohol and drugs are amazing.) Or the time I cut my finger in the kitchen very badly and Dan had had to drive me to the Emergency Medical Service.

But the central message at St. Mary's was, "There is hope here. If you will listen to what we say, you have a chance to get well."

There were a number of people who came to the hospital from the outside and told their story. We would listen to these stories told three and four times a day, and they were so much like our own that at least we began to feel that we were not the only ones in the world who had been through this. The consistent thread is transgenerational, that if there is alcoholism in your family the predilection for addiction is going to be there. Both my grandfathers were alcoholics, and the predilection for addiction is in my children and will be in my grandchildren. The difference is that I know it, and my children know it, and my grandchildren will know it, so they will have a chance.

The first week of treatment I was still traumatized. I didn't have to go through detoxification; my disease was not that advanced, and there was no indication of physical impairment like an enlarged liver. But I was still in a state of shock, and there was still a lot of fear. And, as had been my habit, I was already projecting into what was going to

207

happen when I got home. Whether David would be there.

After about a week I thought, "Why am I resisting this? There will never be another time in my life when I'm given a month to reflect on who I am and what I'm about, and what a rare gift this is. Why not look at it like a gift, treat it as a gift, use it as an opportunity to sort things out."

So in all the lectures and meetings, which really were on-going, I decided to be like a sponge. I would sit there and absorb it all. I wasn't studying. I decided not to work at it really hard the way I had done everything else all my life, but I would allow it to happen, almost rolling around in it. I figured that what really mattered would stick, and what didn't would fall away.

In the evenings we usually went to an AA meeting that was held in the hospital or we would have a lecture or film in which they taught you the intellectual side of alcoholism, and told you they understood the emotional side.

I was in there with teenagers who were addicted to mari-juana, one black-leather-jacketed guy who was a heroin addict, women with a double addiction of Valium and alcohol, airline pilots who were addicted to downers and uppers and alcohol. And we were all the same. It didn't make any difference what the drug was, we were all the same. Addiction is a great leveler.

I'm sure some of those people made it and some didn't. But I will tell you this: anybody who has been through treatment and uses drugs or drinks again is either going to die or is going to come back for more treatment. There is no way that you can ever enjoy an addictive substance again once you know what they teach you in those hospitals.

The killer thing about the disease is that it progresses whether you drink or not. It's a peculiar thing to me, and needless to say I haven't tested it, but if you drink a certain amount and then stop drinking, the amount of alcohol that you will need in order to produce the same effect *progresses* with the period of time. In other words, when people fall off the wagon and start drinking again, they hit it very hard because they have to have as much alcohol as they used to consume *plus* more for the intervening period.

The week before I was released was Family Week, which everyone dreads like the plague. It's a terribly difficult and emotional time, when families confront their own addictions, when nonpatients come and confront one-on-one how they contributed to their family member's disease and how their behavior is directly related to the alcoholic's behavior.

Therapist Sharon Wegscheider has described the dysfunctional family as a mobile. (I thought of our family as an Alexander Calder mobile.) It is perfectly balanced, and if you jerk one of those mobile pieces out of line, all of the rest dangle and move and jangle discordantly, trying to find balance with that one disruptive element. The alcoholic malfunctions, and everything around her malfunctions, scurrying to make sense of the out-of-balance family member. In some ways, co-dependency is more insidious than alcoholism because it's harder to see, it's harder to know what action to take to correct it. Thankfully, there are increasing numbers of programs to help the children of alcoholics. The untreated child of an alcoholic can carry the vestiges of the illness for a lifetime. ACOA, the Adult Children of Alcoholics, is a growing group in the country.

My whole family came for Family Week. We played a game called "sculpting." It's an exercise in which family members literally take other family members and place their arms and legs and entire bodies into shapes and stances, finally arriving at a "sculpture" of the family as they see it.

My children placed me in a chair with my arms upraised and my hands in fists. In their eyes I had succeeded in what I had worked so hard to be, and that was Superwoman. But that was the last place in the world that I wanted to be, and the last thing I wanted them to think of me. Even though my friends might doubt it, I have tried very hard to get out of that chair.

In the hospital I also learned a lot about spirituality. I found a better understanding of my need to commune with a higher power; with God. I relaxed with the idea that there is a spirit and a power that is greater than myself, and that if I will call on and work with that power there will be moments in my life when I will experience true serenity. They may not last long, but they will be worth the effort. I don't think you can truly love yourself or your family or your friends until you accept some concept of the universality of love, that the more you give away the more you get back.

I had seen the very bottom of life. There was no one worse than I had been. The thing I had going for me was that now I knew it. I quit living life in the future. I tried very hard not to ask What-Comes-Next questions—and it goes against my nature, because I really want to know. I stopped living in what I'm going to do next weekend, what I'm going to do next vacation, what I'm going to do next year; I began to live in what is now.

In that hospital I learned that the world is going to get along just fine without me directing it. My children are going to survive, in fact they are going to be better off for having made their own decisions and led their own lives. My responsibility is to love them without question. And by and large they don't want anything more from me than that.

Recovery from alcoholism takes a long, long time. It's a lifelong process. You're in a continuing state of recovery. Not too long ago I was at a friend's house and I was leaning on the back of a chair and another friend was drinking vodka, which was what I used to drink. I smelled the vodka and my impulse was to knock it out of her hand. It smelled like DDT. I wanted to say, "Don't you know that you're poisoning yourself?!" But I didn't.

I was so afraid that I wouldn't be funny anymore. I just knew that I would lose my zaniness and my sense of humor. But I didn't. Recovery turned out to be a wonderful thing. It is absolutely joyous to get up in the morning and feel good, to see the beauty of things around you, to have a life that isn't anesthetized, that's open to all feelings. All of the dastardly, awful things that I feared so much would be found out about me didn't materialize.

I didn't know what I was coming home to, but the important thing was I knew that whatever happened, I could deal with it. In October 1980, shortly after I left the hospital, I asked all my friends, all of the ones who had participated in the intervention, to come over to the house. I wanted to try and explain to them what had taken place at the hospital, how much what they had done had meant to me. I wanted to answer their questions, because I knew they had a million, and I wanted them to know that I didn't want them to feel uncomfortable around me, that their drinking was not going to affect me. My job was to take care of me and their job was to take care of them.

I was their first experience with Life After Alcohol. Most people don't know that you're still going to be you.

We had a long discussion that day about what it meant politically. All of them said that I absolutely could not say to the press or anyone in public life where I had been or what I had been doing. I told them I thought that was ridiculous, that it made no difference to me at all. But they said, "Oh, please do not do that. Just say you have been away taking care of some medical problems." Even though I thought it was pretty silly, that's what I did.

Things with David had not improved. They weren't worse, and I was better able to deal with them, but again our lives were drastically altered. I didn't want to leave work and go to the Raw Deal and sit and drink beer for several hours and listen to everyone get wise. So our whole pattern of living changed, and I think that was very hard on him.

David and I separated for the first time in December of that year, just a few months after I came home. All the children were home for Christmas and what was usually a morning of tre-

211

mendous fun and anticipation was not an easy time. It's funny, I have such a convenient memory, I block out all of those really painful things.

We stayed separated for a very short time. He came home and we agreed that we wanted to try to make a go of it. I still loved him very much—I still do—but I think we were hanging on to what had been, not what is.

I was seeing a counselor who was an alcoholic and understood alcoholism, and I tried to wrestle through the marriage in these sessions. I felt that I had myself pretty well in hand. David said that he would find a marriage counselor for us, and I think he picked someone from the Yellow Pages. I don't remember her name. At one of our sessions she suggested that I prepare a candlelight dinner and that we go dancing; I got kind of tickled. The end result was that it did not work. I think about it and I don't think that it could ever have worked. While I have very serious regrets for the way things were, I can say that I tried very hard.

We separated again that summer, and we were finally divorced in 1984. We had as amicable a divorce as I think people can have.

I was very concerned about the kids and the fact that they had been through so much with me, and then had to deal with this divorce. And while they were older, I knew that it was going to be tough on them because David and I were not just a couple, we were an institution. And it was hard, but they survived it.

I didn't want a parting where the kids felt badly about either one of us, because no matter what, I was going to be their mother for the rest of their lives and David was going to be their Daddy.

By the time the divorce was final we had been married thirty years.

13

★

GETTING a divorce was the hardest thing I have ever done. Harder than alcoholism, harder than treatment, harder than politics. I had never lived alone in my life. Ever. At first I was terribly lonely. I didn't quite fit socially; most of my friends still led virtually the same lives they had led before, and while I was happy to go to parties and gatherings, I was ready to leave by the time the wisdom started getting profound. Which is usually around eight o'clock. I had always said that I never heard anything worth repeating after ten o'clock anyway. Now I scaled that back to about eight or nine.

I spent a lot of time alone. I discovered that there is a difference in being lonely and being alone. I read all the books—*Adjusting to Life After Marriage*, all those things—but somehow they really didn't help a lot. I got comfortable by myself. I had faith that God was going to see me through this thing and that I could survive. Being alone became almost like a treasure. The kids were in and out. Ellen had gone away to school in the Northeast and she would come home in the summertime; Clark would come and go; Dan was there at odd times and that was always fine.

One Saturday morning in late January the phone rang and

woke me up. It was Bob Armstrong, who was in the process of running for governor. Bob asked if I had seen the morning paper. I said, no, I hadn't, I wasn't up yet. He said, "Go get your morning newspaper and call me back."

I went out and got the paper, brought it inside, and called Bob. I said, "Well, I have the newspaper but I don't know why you wanted me to get it."

"Do you see the front page?"

"Yes."

"Warren Harding is in trouble."

Warren Harding was the state treasurer. Warren G. Harding. He was indeed in trouble; the newspaper said a filing cabinet had been seized by the Public Integrity Unit of the district attorney's office, and Harding and ten of his employees had been subpoenaed to testify before the grand jury.

"I see the story," I said. "So, what's up?"

"I want you to run for state treasurer."

I said, "Well, Bob, you're crazy." There were a jillion reasons why I couldn't run for state treasurer. First, I didn't know anything about it. I didn't even know what the job entailed.

Bob said, "Listen, if Warren Harding has been treasurer, you can be treasurer. We are going to be in a fix if Warren Harding really is in serious trouble and is indicted; it will be an embarrassment to have him on the Democratic ticket. And I think it's time for a woman to run statewide."

I said, "Bob, you're really nice and I'll think about it, but I just think that's absurd."

Good grief, here I was, I had just gotten out of the hospital for alcoholism roughly a year before, I was separated from my husband, I was a woman living alone. Any of those by itself would have been enough to defeat me.

Cathy Bonner called. Bob must have called her. She said,

214

"Oh, it's a great idea. Great idea!" Then Liz Carpenter called. Liz said, "You've just got to do this. What a great idea. What a great thing for women."

I said, "Look, Liz, forget the great thing for women. Whatever I do, it has to be a job that I can do."

"Oh, Ann, you can do anything. Don't worry about that."

The calls came in all day. Bob did a good job. He called back and I finally said, "Okay, I will think seriously about it."

There were a couple of catches. First, the deadline for filing to run for that office was only two days away. And second, I wasn't sure that I was eligible to run. There is a law in Texas that says that if you are serving in county office, you must resign your position to run in a state race. My source of income was my commissioner's job.

That day was a flurry of activity. I called Jane Hickie, Claire Korioth, Mary Beth Rogers, Cathy Bonner, Bob Bullock. I called Bill Hobby, who was also on the ticket, and said, "I'm thinking about running for treasurer, what do you think?" Bill was a little surprised, but he said, "Yeah, if you want to do that, that's fine."

By that evening I agreed that we would start the next day, Sunday, and if in twenty-four hours we could get $200,000 pledged to us to make the race, I would take a run at it.

We drew up a list of people I had to talk to: Harry Hubbard, of the AFL-CIO; Howard Rose, the principal lobbyist for the bankers; Gaylord Armstrong; and, of course, David Richards. If I made this race and had to resign as county commissioner, David would have to support me through nine months of campaigning, one whole pregnancy.

By and large, the response was terrific. A bunch of friends got on the phone and started calling around and we had the $200,000 before the end of the day. I pretty well had my feet in the fire.

I called Suzanne Coleman and said, "Suzanne, I need to know what the treasurer does." Suzanne said she would do some research and find out. The next day I went to her house and she sat me down and gave me a briefing.

A number of people began calling, telling us things that they felt we needed to know. Things like the fashion in which banks made contributions to Warren Harding's campaign. One banker would receive a list of the banks in town, the amount of state money deposited in each of those banks, and the total amount of state money in those towns. The amount of money those towns were supposed to raise for Harding was broken down by percentage according to how much state money each bank had. This was on paper. Stupid. Really stupid. There may not have been anything illegal about it, but it was really dumb. I'm sure some towns cooperated and some towns didn't.

Every approved depository bank in the state of Texas— about 1,400 of them—had five thousand dollars of state funds in them, drawing no interest. Again, this was incredibly stupid. I mean, it wasn't enough money to make a difference to any of them, but put together the state was losing interest on seven million dollars a year.

We understood that the interest rate earned on state money was set by a depository board, which seemed to use as a yardstick how their eggs were cooked that morning. There was no rhyme or reason for the way in which it was done.

Suzanne gave me the briefing and the next day I got on a plane and did a nine-city tour announcing my candidacy and what I was going to do as treasurer.

The greatest thing was that the press really didn't know what the treasurer did any more than anyone else did. It had been one of those offices where old elephants went to die. You became treasurer and hoped that nobody would realize you were there. If no one bothered you, you could stay forever.

The Democratic primary was in May and the general election in November, so between the first of February and the first week of May we had to put a campaign together. We had lists, but we didn't even have a computer. What we did have was volunteers. People were coming out of the woodwork to help.

I needed someone to travel with me. I called my son Dan, who had an apartment not far from my home, and asked if I could come talk to him. He said yes.

When I got there I said, "Dan, I need a man to travel with me in this campaign. Are you willing to give me the next nine months of your life?" He said, without hesitation, yes, he was.

That was a real joy. Dan was twenty-two, and there are not very many times that you get to spend an intense period of time with one of your grown children, much less a boy. And he was very good at what he did. He was a very adept advance man; he kept up with the people that we went to see, he would stay right at my elbow in crowds; he would whisper in my ear, "Miss Jones is coming up on your right," and, "Here's Mr. Smith, who we missed seeing the last time," and, "You remember that old drunk man that was here before, well, he's on his way over again."

We would get back to the Holiday Inn without having had any food and he would go across the street and get whatever was available, fried chicken or a fish sandwich, and we would sit on the bed and eat at midnight. Then we'd get up at six in the morning and hit it again.

We mailed every list we could get our hands on. My favorite was the one that started, "Dear Arabian Horse Lover."

The tough part of the campaign was raising money, the mother's milk of politics; you have to have it. Before the campaign was over it had cost over a million dollars. I was personally in debt for about $400,000. We would pay it off with money we brought in at fund-raisers.

217

Politics is a very big and expensive business. Our general routine was that we would lay out a route over a series of towns; David Butts was pretty much responsible for that. I've known him for years and he's a very good friend. We would go into those towns and what they could set up in advance, they did. They would try to have some event where I could meet "people who mattered," it might be a neighborhood group or bankers—bankers are the ones who care the most about who the treasurer is—or some of the women I had met when I had taught workshops over the years.

I would go to the newspaper and ask to speak to the editor. We would try to get a newspaper story or editorial of some kind, we would go to the radio stations, and the television station if there was one. We would set up a press conference, and if they didn't come then we would go to their place to try to get on the news.

Cecile was living in New Orleans and working as a union organizer with the Service Employees International. I called her and said, "Cecile, I really need you." She said, "Okay, I'll come home." She took a leave and got her assignment. She took off by herself in the car, stayed at people's houses to save money, and hit one town after another. I got one editorial endorsement in a town that I had never been in, she was so good. She and Dan took a trip together where they would go in and be interviewed on the radio station.

The primary field consisted of Warren Harding, me, a man named John Cutright from Austin, and a friend of mine from Waco named Lane Denton. The campaign had been going on for about a month and I was in Tyler, in East Texas, when I got a call from the office reporting that Lane Denton had just hosted a press conference at the capitol. Mr. Denton had informed the press that I was an alcoholic, that I had been treated for alcoholism, that I had a mental disorder, and that I had sought counseling for my mental problems.

Appearing at the press conference with Lane Denton was David Samuelson, one of my fellow county commissioners who was no longer in office. I'm paraphrasing, but Samuelson said essentially that my behavior on the court was poor, erratic, and that something was wrong with me.

Well, of course the phones lit up and I had to return all these press calls. I told them that, yes, I certainly was an alcoholic and I had received treatment and was in recovery, and felt very positive about that.

For the next week Lane Denton had my itinerary, and he would go to a town just before I got there, so every time I set foot anywhere these issues and accusations were on the radio, in the newspapers, and were the only questions that I was asked.

The truth of the matter was that those were the questions that I knew how to answer best. I felt sort of sad about having to go through the whole process in public, but I didn't feel devastated. That was the important lesson of treatment: I would survive whatever came.

It was tough on my kids. Really tough. Dan was furious—he's very protective of me anyway. Cecile was outraged. Clark and Ellen were away at school, and so they didn't feel the full brunt of it.

But there was an amazing reaction. An editorial cartoon appeared in the *Austin American-Statesman* and portrayed Lane Denton as a slug. (I think Cecile owns that cartoon.) What was intended as a scandalous revelation was turned to my favor by the fact that I didn't run and hide from it. It was too bad, but if people voted against me because I had a disease and was an alcoholic, so be it. I had to accept who I was, and I had to accept the fact that not all people would accept me the way I was.

Lane Denton received a minimal number of votes and John Cutright got even fewer. I was in a runoff with Warren Harding, and within days after the primary election Warren Harding withdrew. It would have cost us another two or three hundred thousand dollars that we didn't have if we'd had to go through that run-off, but Harding had been indicted and just didn't want to go through another battle. I was the Democratic Party candidate for treasurer.

The man the Republicans chose to run against me was a former Green Beret with some banking experience named Allen Clark. He had lost his legs in the Vietnam War and he was campaigning mostly on his war record. He would come into a town and find a military site, a memorial or airfield or depot, and he would try to gather the press and place a wreath. His wife walked behind him carrying a tape recorder that played "The Ballad of the Green Berets."

No woman had won statewide office in fifty years, and I was hell-bent on breaking that string. I campaigned all over the state, hit all the big cities and a lot of the small towns. Sometimes I'd speak to large crowds, but mostly it was small rooms full of people. I felt that if you get to anybody and they would be still and listen to you, you had a shot at them. We would work the squares of those little towns, go from one store to another talking to people. Almost all of them were enthusiastic.

I thought I knew Texas pretty well, but I had no notion of its size until I campaigned it. One morning I had coffee in Texarkana and had to be at a barbecue in Kingsville that afternoon at five o'clock. We borrowed a little single-engine plane from some kind soul—the people who are just dying to loan a candidate for treasurer a plane are few and far between— and we flew all day. There wasn't any changing planes in airports; there's no down time here—I'm talking about flat flying time; we stayed inside of Texas and we flew *all day*.

The Democratic ticket in 1982 was Lloyd Bentsen for senator; Mark White for governor; Bill Hobby, lieutenant governor; Jim Mattox, attorney general; Garry Mauro, land commissioner; Jim Hightower, agriculture commissioner; and me. Mostly the candidates traveled and campaigned individually, but toward the end we had a caravan.

We had a van that was the funniest thing you have ever seen in your life. I don't know where they found it, but the rumor was that it had belonged to Dinah Shore. It was not a huge touring bus, it was more like one of those vans you see parked at Arby's. There was a bed, and a table, and some built-in couches, and in the back there was a square bathtub with a skylight.

We had all our bumper stickers and signs and brochures stashed in that tub, and at each stop we'd grab a handful and head into the crowds. The guy who was driving was named Jim Swift; he has since died, but he was a great guy. A couple of weeks from the end of the campaign we drove under a low bridge and dispensed with the skylight. Sheared the bubble right off. And of course it rained. It rained right into the tub and over all our material, a total, total waste. By the time we returned that van we couldn't close the front door; there were dents; it was a vintage RV.

We were going from town to town during another part of the campaign and we were traveling in a truck with a loudspeaker on it. You flicked a little switch and whatever you said just boomed out all over South Texas. Dan and Cecile and I were on tour and we pulled up beside this guy parked at a light. He was sitting there, minding his own business, waiting for the light to change, picking his nose. Cecile thought the microphone was off. She broke into her best political barker routine: *"Get your finger out of your nose and come on down to the barbecue this afternoon and see Ann Richards running for treasurer!"*

Well, this poor guy nearly broke his arm getting his finger out of his nose before he gunned his car away from the light!

★　★　★

Bill Hobby was on that ticket and he is one of my favorite people. Hobby has deep roots in Texas politics. His father, William P. Hobby, was governor of Texas from 1917 to 1921 and was instrumental in helping women in Texas get the vote. The Houston airport is named after him. Hobby's mother, Oveta Culp Hobby, had been commanding officer of the Women's Army Corps and became the second woman to serve in a presidential cabinet when she served as Secretary of Health, Education and Welfare under President Eisenhower. She later was president-editor of the *Houston Post*.

Bill was brought up in a household in which there was a great deal of domestic help, I assume, and he is hardly skilled at what one would call householding. His wonderful wife, Diana, has always seen to Bill's every need. I've been there when Diana would come in and say, "Bill, will you be needing the down jacket?" And I would say, "What are you doing?!"

"I'm going hunting tomorrow," Bill would tell me.

Diana would be putting together his hunting gear and I would pitch a fit. "Diana, what in the world are you doing? He can perfectly well put his own stuff together to go hunting."

Bill and Diana were very generous to me. When I was campaigning in Houston I stayed with them at their beautiful old house on South Boulevard. It was Saturday night, about two weeks before the election, and Bill and I were scheduled to visit a number of black churches the next morning.

It was cold that night and rather than put their dogs out, Bill and Diana let them stay in the kitchen. (The Hobbys have four children, all of whom are now grown, and at one time or another they acquired dogs. Big dogs. As the kids left home, Diana, dear soul that she is, cared for these animals.) I got up early Sunday morning and went down to make coffee. I opened the swinging door and as I did, I hit a large pile of dog manure on the kitchen floor, and of course spread it partway into the room.

I thought, "My God, I can't deal with this. It's five-thirty in the morning, I'll just go over there and I won't look and I'll make the coffee and then I'll come back and figure out how to handle it."

You know how when you're in a strange house you don't know where anything is, well I was fumbling around in the kitchen when I heard the door squeak. I looked up and the swinging door was beginning to open. I called, "Don't open that door!"

It was Bill, in his pajamas and his robe, and he of course paid no attention to what I said. He spread the stuff all the way across the kitchen floor as if the door were a trowel. I said, "Bill, the dogs have messed. I'm going to make the coffee and I'll clean it up as soon as I get through."

Now Hobby is not long on talking, so while I'm over there putting the coffee together he goes to the laundry room and comes back with a bucket of water and a pressed tea towel, and in all seriousness hands it to me. I'm not sure that he didn't know that you couldn't clean up a pile of dog manure with a washed and ironed tea towel. And I'm sure never going to let him forget it.

What really made the difference in that campaign was the fact that Lloyd Bentsen was at the top of the ticket. His organization has the reputation of being one of the best in politics, and I got a chance to see firsthand that it was.

Good organizations have to be nurtured and fed, and Lloyd Bentsen has done a superb job. His county coordinators take their jobs not as an honor but as a responsibility. A lot of these people have been with Lloyd from the very beginning and they are with him to the end. Lloyd keeps in touch, he keeps his

223

people informed, and they know what to do. From the state's largest cities to the small towns of East Texas, if you go in there, there will be a crowd—because Lloyd Bentsen's coordinator will have turned out a crowd.

A lot of politicians make the mistake of not continuing to build an organization once they have assumed power. Lloyd has established a network of people in every county who will work for him when it's time to go to work, and who will care about him in the off-season. That takes a gentle touch and years of service. Between elections his machine is dormant, but it can be energized and exercised at any time.

It doesn't work like the ward politics of the big cities, it doesn't dispense patronage, there isn't some cynical *quid pro quo*. Lloyd may want to get in touch with a coordinator as a matter of courtesy, or because the call will help somewhere along the line, but it isn't necessary. These are people who believe in Lloyd Bentsen because he has come through for them and will continue to come through.

Lloyd is a very good negotiator and a tough trader. He is very bright and has had the good judgment to build a staff of people around him who are smart and effective. Any time you see truly successful public officials you know they have excellent staff, and that reflects back on them.

Lloyd is not your typical politician. He has a very loyal core of workers, not just county coordinators but people he has kept in touch with over the years, who will not only turn out if he comes to their hometown for an event but who will get on a bus and ride to Houston if their presence is required. They will literally go the extra mile for Lloyd Bentsen.

Lloyd has been in the United States Senate eighteen years. A lot of business gets transpired, bases get touched, connections get made in eighteen years. He is tremendously effective in a room of power brokers. For a man of his breeding and manicured looks he is very casual, very informal. He will stand up before them and briefly review whatever current legislation is on the minds of the people, he will tell them what he thinks about it and where it is going. He will then talk briefly about his campaign and where it is going, and how much he needs their help, and that's about it. There is no strong-arm operation there. I think the word that best describes Lloyd Bentsen's political operation is *gentlemanly*.

When the extension of the Equal Rights Amendment was coming up for a vote, Liz Carpenter, Owanah Anderson, Jane Hickie, and I went to lobby him. We put on every piece of fine jewelry we owned and were dressed to the nines, and Liz had brought along an umbrella and was stomping along tapping it in the hallway. We really wanted his support.

Lloyd expressed some concern about the extension and what precedent it might set, and Liz got upset. She banged her cane on the floor and said mightily, "Lloyd Bentsen, you are a stubborn Swede!"

And Lloyd, in his calm way, said, "Liz, I'm a Dane."

"Well, okay, you're a stubborn Dane!"

But we did all right. We got his support.

I won the election with 61.4 percent of the vote. I was treasurer of the state of Texas. Now I had to do the job.

14

★

MY immediate task was to put together a group of people who wanted to work at the Treasury. And I want to emphasize *wanted*. One of the keys to a successful operation is that the people who are there want to be there; people work best doing what they want to do. The next task was to screen the present employees and determine which of them wanted to stay, and which were worth keeping.

We put together a rather elaborate interview process. Jane Hickie, Chula Reynolds, and Stuart Vexler were the principal interviewers, and they talked to the employees and asked for recommendations. People are very forthcoming if you tell them their words will be held in confidence; all you have to do is ask them.

There were two key positions: chief of operations, someone who could run the money side of the agency; and deputy treasurer, someone who could act as number two to me and deal with the personnel structure, purchasing, general management, and all of the problems and nuances that occur.

I had gone to Mary Beth Rogers and asked if she would give me just a little of her time to put together the Women's History Project, and she came out from under it four years later. She had once worked under Bob Armstrong at the General Land Office, and I could think of no one more ideal as second-in-command than Mary Beth. After I had done some convincing, she accepted.

I called around to a number of bankers for recommendations and found a young banker/accountant named Paul Williams. I met him and within three days we had an apartment rented for him and he had moved in. He has been a godsend. He runs the money side of the Treasury, directing the investment of funds; cash management, the money flow, making sure we have adequate cash on hand to meet the bills as they come due; the accounting, making sure that our numbers reconcile with the comptroller's.

I don't want to make this complicated, because when you talk about money most people's eyes roll back in their heads and there becomes some sort of blood block so it can't reach their brain until you get through talking about it. But to put it simply: money is a commodity; there are people who want to buy it and will pay you good money for it. Basically they're renting it for a while, because they may see an opportunity to take your money and make more money than they are paying you for it.

The state Treasury takes all the revenue of the state of Texas, pays the state's bills, and invests the rest. So that you can understand the magnitude of the Treasury, that means we pay over 12 million state warrants and deposit over eight million checks annually. The total amount of money coming and going is almost $80 billion. The average amount we have invested on a daily basis is over $25 billion. We also hold over $30 billion in securities owned by various state agencies in our vault and we collect over $350 million in cigarette taxes.

The state Treasury does business with over 1,400 banks in the state, making us second only to the federal government in the number of banking relationships maintained by a governmental body. Our banking relationships have also been one of our greatest challenges. Anyone who reads about Texas knows that we have experienced over 250 bank failures in the last six and a half years. As a result of overhauling the system used by the Treasury to monitor the safety of our bank deposits, we have not lost one penny in state deposits in a failed bank.

I had campaigned all over the state, saying that the Treasury was a mess, that we needed to bring it into the twentieth century. When we got down there we could not believe it. The men doing the calculating might just as well have been wearing arm garters and green eyeshades.

There were boxes of checks sitting in drawers—shoe boxes of them, some of them months old. The Treasury was processing about 30,000 checks totaling $100 million a day on ten-key adding machines. Checks would come in and the staff would add them up, wrap them in the adding machine tape, and put a rubber band around the whole thing. It would take from two to three days just to get the checks into the bank.

Now remember, people will pay you to let them use your money, so for two or three days these checks were in our possession but not our bank account and the people of Texas were losing an opportunity to make money.

It became immediately obvious that we needed to go to the legislature to ask them to buy the equipment necessary to process the checks and speed that money to the bank. Mark White had been elected governor, and through an emergency appropriation and a lot of convincing, within about five months we were able to order the equipment. With the additional money we made, we paid for that equipment in about two weeks.

We knew how long it took us to get money into the bank, and so the next logical question was, How long does it take other agencies to get money to the Treasury? How much time and money were we losing there? I called Garry Mauro, who had just been elected to the Land Office, and asked, "Garry, how long does it take to get checks from your office to mine?" He said he didn't know, he'd just gotten there, but he would find out. He called down and found that the Land Office, which collected sizable sums from leases on state-owned lands, some of them oil-producing, delivered money to the Treasury *when the bag got full.* And we were literally across the street from each other.

We got the picture. We established a section in the Treasury called Rapid Deposit, and custom-designed processing systems through which other agencies could get money to us faster. Currently the Rapid Deposit programs we have in place speed over $1 billion into the Treasury, have earned almost $6 million in additional interest, and have saved agencies using the program almost as much in personnel and equipment costs.

When you pay your bills, many times your return envelope has a post office box as an address. More often than not, that post office box is a lockbox in a bank. The receiver makes arrangements with the financial institution: in return for putting that lockbox in their bank, they will start giving interest at a specific time on the arrival of those checks.

Starting at five o'clock in the morning or earlier, the bank will take the receipts from the box and enter the credit to your account. They will then process the payment information for you. They will continue to visit the box regularly all day, providing a steady stream of income. So the checks do not pile up and we don't have to go through a complex bookkeeping operation; the money starts earning interest the minute it hits the lockbox.

In some of the larger agencies, such as a Highway Department office in a small town, we found they would receive money for fees from driver's licenses and such, and run it through their whole bookkeeping system, then send that money and a copy of their records to the regional office, which would repeat the process and send it on to the state office, which would repeat the whole process one more time. Eventually, a week to three weeks later, the money would arrive at the Treasury.

Well, it was pretty simple for the Treasury to open accounts at banks in every one of those towns—and, where possible, in close proximity to the state office—and every day when the staff leaves, they deposit the checks. They then make a toll-free call to report the deposit, which is electronically transmitted to our computer. The computer processes a tape that goes to the Federal Reserve and sweeps all of that day's deposits into the Treasury's main account the following day.

The Treasury creates more electronic banking entries, in both volume and total dollars, than any other entity in the state. Our ability to use new technologies has allowed us to provide more services at less cost to state government.

There were a lot of agencies that didn't understand that if there is something wrong with a check, or if there is some question about the amount of money—either over or under what it's supposed to be—it can be put in a suspense account and earn interest until the problem has been resolved. Essentially I think that's why we were finding all those checks lying around in boxes; there was some question, and rather than put the checks in a suspense account and let them earn money, the old regime just stuck them in a drawer and figured they would puzzle them out when they had the time. It was amazing to me, but this was the way the state of Texas had handled its money.

The major funds of Texas buy and sell a lot of securities, and one of the first weeks we were there the Teachers' Retirement Fund called over on a Thursday and said that they would need $60 million the following day to make a security purchase. That was when we discovered that there was no cash-flow analysis for the state at all. It was just by guess and by God. The previous generation of treasurers had maintained a lot of non-interest-bearing accounts to be able to pull the cash together to meet this kind of demand in case it came. Again, the people of Texas were losing money.

We began working with these major funds, asking them to lay out a schedule of their expected purchases. We weren't asking them to tell us any secrets, or to make purchases at our convenience; all we wanted was a vague notion of what they were going to do and when they were going to do it, so we could have the money on hand for them. We got it refined to weekly and then daily reports that track money coming and going into over two hundred different state funds, so ultimately we had a real handle on when money was going to be needed. If it wasn't going to be needed, we could invest it in accounts for longer durations that paid higher rates. We put money into 180-day accounts for the first time when I became treasurer.

The ability to forecast the state's cash flow also allowed the Treasury to foresee a cash-flow crisis. We convinced the legislature to authorize us to issue short-term notes to meet the state's obligations which allowed employees to get paid on time and schools to open as scheduled.

In the process of bringing the agency into the twentieth century we greatly expanded the investment authority of the Treasury. The cumulative effect has been over $1.3 billion in interest earned on the Treasury's investments.

We also began the serious enforcement of the unclaimed-property laws. Simply stated, if you abandon property, or forget about it, or die, and no one claims that property—money in banks, oil royalties, various kinds of stock investments—after a certain period of time it is turned over to the state. The state's obligation is to hold that property until you or your heirs claim it—in perpetuity.

We aggressively try to find the property owners by collating all the names turned over to us by the banks and savings and loans and oil companies. We then attempt to locate the rightful owners. We publish about a hundred thousand names every year in a tabloid advertisement that comes out in the Sunday newspaper. But during the time that the state has this unclaimed property, the state is able to make use of it and makes money on it. Since I have been treasurer we have returned over $92 million to rightful owners. And we have made $223 million for the state. The Treasury sells tax stamps for cigarettes. It is a $350-million-a-year business. When we arrived, the accounts were kept in a Boston ledger with a #2 lead pencil. We have computerized the operation of cigarette tax stamp collection which has speeded operations and increased accountability.

The position of an elected official is really an executive management job. Elected officials at the state level are like directors of very large corporations; no one has the time to devote to full-time hands-on minute-to-minute oversight. I cannot emphasize enough what a valuable group of people I have working with me. I hope that I, in turn, have made the Treasury a good place to work.

It is also very important to me that we have done such a good job with a great number of minorities and women on the staff. If there is any place that should reflect the population it is government, and we have exceeded those numbers at the Treasury. The Texas Treasury is a working example of blacks and Hispanics and women, as well as Anglo men, working together and doing a superb job.

By the time I complete my second term of office we will have made more money in eight years than all the previous treasurers—combined—in the 146-year history of the state of Texas. Not saved; *made*. And mind you, every dollar that I earn at the Treasury is one less dollar that the people have to pay in taxes. We will probably top out at about one billion, eight hundred million dollars.

Elected officials are very busy people, and during a legislative session they are being asked to understand more issues than they can possibly say grace over. As treasurer, I was often called upon to encourage elected officials to pass legislation I considered necessary or worthwhile. I can't use the word lobby, because state agencies are not allowed to lobby members of the legislature. We are, however, permitted to provide information, and I provide the legislators with information myself. That's not always done.

I have never quite understood protocol. There is all this business of who goes to see whom according to the rank and prestige of office. Do you go to see them or do you ask them to come and see you? I've always thought such posturing was stupid and artificial and silly. I don't understand it and I don't practice it. I just thought it was important that these guys really got to know me and understand me, and know that I was not going to sell them some mess of pottage.

One of the tough pieces of legislation to pass was a bill that would have required health insurers in Texas to cover the treatment of alcoholism and drug abuse. A number of my friends are in recovery and one of these friends, Robert Spellings, was taking the lead to try to get this legislation through. There are an awful lot of people out there who need treatment, and a lot of them don't have insurance, but the ones who do certainly ought to be covered. I had found the situation within my own agency, where I had employees who had a drug or alcohol problem; it was much easier to talk to them and get them into treatment if they had insurance to cover it. Treatment is not cheap, the cost is dear. It was $10,000 when I went through it, and that was nine years ago. Some nonprofit centers like the Betty Ford Center charge $6,000, but the for-profit hospitals charge much more.

Initially the insurance industry said that requiring drug- and alcohol-treatment coverage was going to drive premiums up and cost more people more money. Well, we had the numbers, chapter and verse, showing the high cost of treatment of other illnesses which are the direct result of alcohol and drug abuse: broken arms, broken legs, stomach disorders, liver disease. The statistics are pretty clear that if you treat the primary illness—addiction—the other doctor visits and hospitalizations will go away.

I testified before the committee and told them that I have hardly been sick a day since my treatment; I used to be sick with one thing or another all the time. Comptroller Bob Bullock, who had also been through treatment and is a recovering alcoholic, also spoke before the committee. It was pretty powerful, two elected government officials testifying to the benefits out of their own experience.

It was a tussle, but we passed the bill. Unfortunately, in order to get it enacted we had to agree to take drug abuse out of it. The bill that passed requires coverage for alcoholism, but if you are addicted to something other than alcohol, it's not covered. Isn't that ridiculous? At the next session, in the spring of 1989, Senate Bill 911 passed the legislature providing mandatory insurance coverage for chemical dependency.

It was really thrilling for me—it still is thrilling for me—to see those bills pass, to see things like that happen. I'm a great believer in synergism, the idea that things are greater than the sum of their parts. There is a synergism when people come together in a common purpose that creates a powerful force. People are capable of so much more than they think they are; they begin to believe in their own abilities when they are around people who believe in them.

That's not to say that there are not specious pieces of legislation, and legislators who are playing to the most base instincts. But by and large that stuff gets washed out; it may make headlines, but it doesn't become law.

There's an old saying that there are two things you should never see made: legislation and sausage. But while it is a difficult and stressful time, the legislative drive is also one of the most

exhilarating. It doesn't get old to know that you are partici-
pating in a process that for the most part is going to make
people's lives better.

During my second year at the Treasury I left the Red Bud Trail
house. It was a great big old five-bedroom, five-bathroom house
and I was rambling around in it all by myself. I loved the house
and the place too much to let it run down, so I started looking
for another place to live. I very shortly found a house that I liked
a lot. It took me a year to buy it, and finally, right before
Christmas 1984, I moved in.

Leaving Red Bud Trail was wrenching. I was closing the
door on a major part of my life, but it also seemed an opportunity to put a lot of grief and bitterness behind me. It was kind
of like closing the lid on Pandora's box. It has taken me some
time but now I think back to the days in that house, and all the
fun and laughter that was there, with a lot of affection and no
regrets.

My new home has its landmark events. Lynn Whitten was
married here. And Cecile was married to Kirk Adams in this
house. They are a wonderful match.

About three years ago Sam Whitten died. It's really difficult when your friends die, as if a piece of you isn't there
anymore and you'll never find it again. Like David and me, Sam
and Virginia were an institution and I think she felt adrift for
a long time. Virginia went through some tough times, but she's
beginning to come into her own now.

Cecile and Kirk had moved to California and were organizing for the Service Employees International Union when
they called and told me Cecile was pregnant. I had never really
thought much about being a grandmother—I don't think that's
something you do think much about—and I was totally unprepared for the way I felt when that child was born.

They named her Lily Anna.

There's something about a grandchild. It's the first time you have the experience of seeing your life stretch beyond you. You don't really see it with your own children, because you're so busy with the direct responsibility of their upbringing. But with a grandchild it is as if you know that your life will go on after you're dead. I was awed by the degree of tenderness and overwhelming love I felt for that child. It came pouring out of me. There is no other feeling like it. My son Clark married a wonderful woman named Paula and last December they presented me with my second granddaughter, Jennifer, whom I also adore.

Now that I was a statewide elected official I was invited to places and events I'd rarely had access to before. Paul Kirk, National Chair of the Democratic Party, named me to the Steering Committee of the Democratic Policy Commission in May of 1985. Among the policy commission's objectives were to return the Democratic Party to its roots, spotlight its innovations, and communicate its vision for the future. I was pleased and honored to be chosen to participate.

Our first meeting was in Washington, D.C., and the gathering was chaired by Governor Scott Matheson of Utah and attended by, among others, U.S. Representative Marcy Kaptur of Ohio, State Representative Larry Echohawk of Idaho, and Lottie Shackleford, now the mayor of Little Rock, Arkansas. Bob Kerry, who was then governor and is now senator from Nebraska, was there with Debra Winger, whom he was dating at the time. Wisconsin Congressman Les Aspin headed the Defense and Foreign Policy Committee, and I was asked to work on a committee called Family, Community, and Social Justice.

This was the first time I had met Governor Michael Dukakis, and I was impressed. He headed the committee on the

Industrial and Entrepreneurial Economy. Dukakis made a commitment to do a complete analysis with recommendations, as we all had, but he really carried through on his, he really produced. He came back with a thoughtful, substantive report that wasn't all pap. It's easy to blow smoke in the general direction of your topic, but Dukakis gave specific instances of programs and ways in which they had worked.

Michael Dukakis was known for a program he had developed in Massachusetts in which low-income women who were trying to raise families, but who had no skills, were trained for jobs and received job placements. He consciously approached the notion of getting people off welfare and into productivity. The generic term is Workfare, and it is now being done in any number of states, but Massachusetts was the front-runner.

The reports of the policy commission's various committees were presented in Atlanta in 1986. I was very taken with Atlanta's Mayor Andrew Young; his enthusiasm for the city of Atlanta is infectious.

When you see these kinds of meetings on television you think there are all of these people sitting around the table deliberating. But the truth is that the reports are pretty much written in private and then circulated so each participant has an opportunity to edit or make suggestions on other people's reports.

I was concerned about the presentation of my section's report. The teacher and legislative wrangler in me wanted to bring to this task force the faces of the people we were talking about. I know I say this often, but it is key: in government we get involved in concepts and universal solutions without really seeing the people whose lives we are affecting.

Usually when these reports are presented to the general body they are read, like book reports in grade school or bills in Congress. We started my report with a black children's choir from Atlanta. We commissioned big blown-up photographs

237

which we mounted on tripods and placed all around the room, pictures of different kinds of families, old and young, all different races and colors. Then, when we had everyone's attention, we said what we had to say.

During this period something happened that seemed of little significance to me at the time. Ben Barnes, who had been lieutenant governor and had run for governor and been defeated, had gone back home to live and work in Brownwood. He and John Connally formed a business relationship and now Ben was moving to Austin. A Ben Barnes Farewell Dinner was being held in Brownwood and I got a call inviting me to participate. It was a roast.

These roasts, in which a man's friends and acquaintances gather affectionately to slander him, had formerly been all-male affairs. To be invited to participate was a fun prospect.

I got up and said, "I am really flattered to be asked to be here tonight, but I know that the reason I am here is that I am one of the few women in Barnes's past who is respectable-enough looking to sit at a head table with all of these men.

"My first work association with Ben Barnes was when I was county commissioner. Barnes was developing some land and he would come in and turn around three or four times, and he would ramble on about one thing or another, and by the time he left you never knew why Barnes was there. He is probably the most affable, likable, charming guy you would ever hope to meet, but with all the round-and-round and back-and-forth and blowing hot air, it's kind of like dealing with an oscillating fan."

Well, his friends knew him and they were hysterical because they knew it was true.

When I had been county commissioner Barnes and Connally had wanted to do a land development and I had insisted that the bridge that led to the development was inadequate for the traffic it would carry, and if Barnes was to go forward he would have to build a new bridge. Barnes was aghast, but the upshot of it was that the bridge was built and it cost him about $250,000. There had been a recent news story about how John Connally and Barnes had gone over to Saudi Arabia to do business, and I told Connally, "If you are putting Ben Barnes in a tent with the Saudis, it is very possible that you are going to be expected to dam the Nile."

I don't know how the word gets out, but suddenly I was invited to speak at any number of roasts. I enjoyed doing them, but I was always worried because there is a general feeling that if you are funny you're not serious. People don't know how many brain cells it takes to be funny. I've watched Jim Hightower cut opponents to shreds with humor. Humor is a powerful tool. It clears the air. Once you laugh, your mind opens and then you are able to hear the other things that are being said to you.

I was also on the more conventional speaking circuit. If you make one good speech to a chamber of commerce then all the other chambers of commerce want you to speak to them. After that roast the demand for speeches became overwhelming. The invitations were running over a dozen a day, and I accepted as many as I could. It became a routine. I was on the road two or three nights a week, usually flying out after work, making the speech, and flying back in late at night.

In the summer of 1984, Walter Mondale invited about thirty women to St. Paul, Minnesota, to discuss the vicepresidential choice, and I was among them. I had met many of these women in organizations or on President Carter's Advisory Committee or at the National Women's Political Caucus. Judy Goldsmith, the president of the National Organization for Women, was there, as were Sharon Percy Rockefeller from Virginia, Carol Bellamy of New York, and Bambi Cardenas from San Antonio. One woman, former Congresswoman Patsy Mink, I had known as far back as the Young Democrats.

When I walked into the room I was amazed to see that the

top Mondale staff was there. It dawned on me that this was a serious meeting; they don't bring their top staff unless what you have to say is going to be heard.

Joan Mondale came in with Fritz. They sat down and he made some opening remarks about how he wanted our feelings and suggestions as to the best choice that could be made for vice president. He told us he wanted each of us, in turn, to talk about the choice that would be best in our individual states.

Almost without exception, each woman named a man. I said that, in Texas, Lloyd Bentsen would undoubtedly be the best choice, and I laid out why: the level of respect felt for him; the impact he had had on the 1982 election; his tremendous organization; his experience and ability.

I believe we were all very truthful with Mondale. We knew there was a possibility that a woman would be nominated, but we wanted to give him our best thinking on what really would benefit the ticket the most in our home states.

NOW and the National Women's Political Caucus were pushing hard for a woman to be chosen. And in the end we all agreed that if there was no man who would make a striking difference to the ticket, choosing a woman would certainly be precedent-setting and a historical event.

You can't imagine how exciting and thrilling it was to have a nominee for president seriously seeking out the advice of women. It had been hard enough to be taken seriously in Travis County, and now there was a real possibility that all across the country people would see a woman in a position of national leadership. When I left that meeting I felt he was going to nominate a woman.

In San Francisco the night Geraldine Ferraro was nominated for vice president, the men in the Texas delegation did a fabulous thing: they allowed the women alternate delegates to come and take their seats on the convention floor. It was a terrific night. The women journalists were thrilled too, and there was a warm, joyous bonding among the women at the convention; we seemed for the moment like one big community.

The people who had done the most work for Mondale in Texas were Buddy Temple, the former railroad commissioner and husband of my friend Ellen, and Calvin Guest, a banker who had been the Texas state chair of the Democratic Party. They had had a meeting with Mondale, and I don't know how it all came about, but Calvin came and told me I was going to be asked to second Mondale's nomination.

Well, I was just stunned. I had no more idea than the man in the moon how to do it or what to say. I went back to my hotel with Cecile and Mary Beth Rogers and we holed up in my room and tried to put a speech together. I wasn't altogether happy with what we produced but I didn't embarrass myself and it was great to have the experience.

I traveled some in the Mondale campaign and did some warm-ups before the candidate and other people spoke. I got to introduce Geraldine Ferraro at a big rally on the steps of the state capitol, and Gerry was well received; people liked her. I was very pleased with my opening remarks, which were essentially, "People ask all the time, will Texans vote for a woman? Well, my Mama didn't call me Bubba!"

Some of the elected officials left Austin to fly with Gerry and Fritz to Houston, where they were to speak at another rally. The national press corps was with us, hundreds of reporters and photographers and cameramen recording everything everyone said. On the plane, Bill Hobby came to my seat and asked, "Ann, do you have that speech that you used to introduce Ms. Ferraro back at the capitol?"

I said, "Yes. What do you want with it?"

"Well, I have to introduce her in Houston."

I gave Hobby my copy of the speech and we got on that platform and Bill Hobby proceeded to read the very same speech that I had just given a couple of hours before in Austin.

While Hobby was speaking, Fritz Mondale leaned over to me and said, "He's giving your speech." I said, "Oh, hush, it's the best speech he's ever given in his life."

I think that tells you a great deal about the strength of Bill Hobby. There are not many politicians who will get up in front of the national press and repeat a speech he knows they just heard someone else give. It takes a person who is truly secure in himself to do that. But he didn't say that his Mama never called him Bubba.

We had a little down time in Texarkana on one trip and I asked Fritz Mondale what the last four years had been like. Because essentially, ever since he had lost as Jimmy Carter's vice-presidential running mate, he had been preparing to run for president. He said that, truthfully, things were just a blur.

"If you ask me about specific events or instances, I recall them and the people involved with clarity. But in general, it's a blur."

I can understand that. The pace demanded of national candidates is simply unbelievable. Because of scheduling and flying in and out of as many as ten or twelve cities a day, it becomes necessary to say the same thing several days running to twenty or thirty different crowds. The physical demands are so great that you cannot stay mentally alert enough to supply different nuances for every crowd. A topical reference suggested by an aide or local coordinator is about as much fresh material as a candidate can be expected to inject. That's why most candidates give the same speech over and over and over again.

The people at the receiving end—the well-wishers and hand-shakers and county coordinators, and all the elected officials waiting for you when you get off that plane—will have a very definitive impression and memory of that moment in time in which the two of you exchange remarks. But for the candidate who is making eight or ten of these stops a day, there's no way. You do well to remember the crowd you saw that morning, much less the one you had seen months before.

I was not really greatly disappointed by the 1984 election results because my hopes for victory were not that high. I do think that Geraldine Ferraro did a remarkable job. When you stop to think that her congressional district was smaller than my county commissioner precinct, and that she was told, "All right, you are the vice-presidential nominee; go out and campaign all over the country," that's no small task. The fact that a woman has now run for that high an office cannot be over-estimated. The path has been opened.

Women have always known that, if given the opportunity, we could do the job. It's just that most jobs, like most everything else, get filled before a lot of the qualified people ever hear about them. Call it the old school tie, good ol' boys, networking, whatever. If the people in charge don't know you, you aren't going to get any time or attention. We set out to change that situation in Texas.

The Foundation for Women's Resources, which funded the Women's History Project, created a program called Leadership Texas. It was based on a program that various communities were doing around the state—Leadership Austin, Leadership San Antonio, Leadership Dallas—in which the chambers of commerce would take young leaders on their way up, expose them to the various facets of the community, and introduce them to the city's leading government and business people. In this way, when the new movers and shakers came along they would be better prepared to assume community responsibilities.

We have learned over the years that one of the things women felt they did not have enough of was "connections." They didn't have enough connections with each other and they didn't have enough access, or connections, to the power brokers and decision makers, whether in business or government or higher education. And so, as bright as they might be and as hard as they might try, women found it very difficult to move ahead.

Leadership Texas really was Cathy Bonner's baby. Just as they had said to me, "Okay, if you take this history project we'll get behind you to do it," we said to Cathy, "Well, if you want to give it a try and put it together, we're all for it."

Our plan was to bring women together from all over Texas and have them visit six Texas cities over a year's time. In each city they would concentrate on the strength of that region or community, and be introduced to the people who made things happen. At the same time they would be exposed to the community's problems and social ills. This wasn't a standard young executive's training course, where all you care about is how to make the next and last dollar; the agenda was wide and the concerns were far-reaching.

The first year, we invited applications and resumes, forms which would tell us who the women were, what their activities had been, and essays about why they wanted to be in the program. We knew it was the right idea, and our concerns weren't about whether or not it would be successful; we were worried about the cost of it. We knew the program was going to be expensive. The first year's fee was $2,000 per person.

We were concerned lest we be dealing only with a group that could afford that kind of tuition, so we went about raising money for scholarships. We hired a really bright woman named Martha Farmer, whose husband was a minister in Austin, and she was a genius at it. She would get corporations to sponsor their employees and pay their tuition, and at the same time to sponsor a scholarship and give us an extra tuition. We had a lot of applicants who couldn't afford to pay, and many of them were able to enter the program this way.

There were no age restrictions, though most of the women

who have gone through Leadership Texas are relatively young, in their thirties or early forties. The first year we took about fifty women and were successful beyond anything we had ever imagined. From then on it just took off.

Texas women needed to know how Texas works. When we took them to Dallas, we presented a whole section on banking. In Houston the women visited with administrators, doctors, and technicians at the Medical Center. They watched open-heart surgery with Dr. Debakey. In West Texas and the high plains they went for afternoon refreshments at Boone Pickens' house. At that same session they heard talks about agriculture and lectures on the problems of water in West Texas. In El Paso they heard from immigration officials about the problems in the border communities. In Austin we introduced them to elected officials.

We worked very hard at being nonpartisan. I was on the board of directors and would speak with the women, and in Dallas they were entertained at the home of Governor Bill Clements.

Well, it was just a natural. Right from the start young women came out of this program who are going to be their communities' leaders tomorrow. As a direct result, these women have begun doing business with each other; a network has been created. The women formed an alumnae association that pays for scholarships so other women can attend. It has become a strong and wonderful thing to see.

Martha Farmer's husband was transferred to a church in Arlington, Virginia, and we were sick to see her leave. We decided that, since we really didn't want to let Martha go, we would take this program national. In 1987 we created Leadership America, and the response has been overwhelming and enthusiastic.

★ ★ ★

245

I thought the 1988 election was the Democrats' to win. When I came home from the national convention in Atlanta I sensed a real enthusiasm and spirit about the campaign; after eight years of torpor at the top, there was the feeling that we could win this one.

And then nothing happened.

I don't remember at what point the coordinator for Texas arrived from Boston, but it was several weeks after the nomination. My office was getting an awful lot of calls for me to make speeches around the country. I knew that my time was limited and I wanted to spend it in the best way possible. Carrying Texas was very important to me, especially since Lloyd Bentsen was on the ticket, so once Texas had a coordinator I asked Jane Hickie to go over and establish with them what they wanted of me. I had a Treasury to run, and obligations I had made long before the spotlight hit me, and I wanted to be sure that we gave the campaign whatever they wanted.

We had already committed to making a couple of trips to New York and to California, and Jane came back from her meeting saying that my obligation was to do those events and to spend at least five days each month traveling for the ticket in Texas. I said I was happy to do that, and I was sure they knew that the more advance notice I was given before travel, the better; the speech requests were coming in like crazy and the volume of mail was enormous.

And then we just didn't hear from the campaign. Jane called back to say that I stood ready to do anything they wanted me to do. That didn't produce anything.

There were other Democrats on the ticket, running for judgeships or Congress or the state legislature, and I resolved to help them. I went on one trip out to East Texas for a fellow named Richard Anderson who was running for reelection to the State Senate. He threw a big fund-raiser and there were a lot

246

of elected officials there: Jim Hightower, Bill Hobby, Senator Hugh Parmer. I think it was Hightower who said, "Well, has the campaign called and asked you all to do anything?"

We all said no.

In the heat of a campaign, things get pretty frantic. I wasn't going to call the national office and say, "They won't let us do anything down here"; that sounds so corny. But I was hearing the same kind of complaints in other states as well.

I went up to New York City for a major fund-raiser being run by Nadine Hack. Nadine is very good and had raised millions of dollars for Dukakis. This particular one was a $5 million deal. It was in the middle of the worst of the Republican media barrage. The Willie Lee Horton furlough stories, the attack on Dukakis over the Pledge of Allegiance—all of that gimmickry was going full tilt.

I had been to New York before and met several contributors, and this time they were all coming up to me and saying, "Ann, we really need you to talk to somebody in Boston. We've got to respond to this stuff."

I thought they had a lot more influence than I did. "Well, look," I told them, "you can tell them yourselves. You've got a big investment in this campaign."

"No. Uh-uh. We feel uneasy about that. We don't know how to do that."

I was scheduled to fly back to Texas the next afternoon when I got a call from the Dukakis office wanting to know if I would go to a rally they were holding in Commerce, Texas. I could fly down there with Dukakis and his staff. I said of course I would.

I was sitting in the limousine next to Michael Dukakis, going out to the airport, and I began to tell him that I really was worried about the way the campaign was going. I told him I thought that he needed to get angry.

247

"I don't know what it takes to make you mad," I told him, "but they are insulting your integrity, your patriotism, your wife. It's justified that you respond in anger."

He told me he would take it under advisement.

I will tell you that I admire Michael Dukakis a lot. I think he would have made an excellent Chief Executive. But I didn't really feel that I was getting through.

I would love to be able to offer an explanation of why we lost, but I think there were so many reasons that no one of them is enough. I think the Republicans did a fantastic job of preparing for the campaign. They did their focus groups early on, so they knew the reaction to the Willie Lee Horton story, they knew the reaction to their manufactured Pledge of Allegiance charge. Before the Republican convention ever took place, they were ready.

Roger Ailes and Lee Atwater did an incredible job, and we were totally unprepared to deal with it. We didn't seem to have a plan that guided the campaign. And those of us who really wanted to help didn't get an opportunity to do it.

I have some pretty strong feelings about why the Democratic Party is finding it difficult to win presidential elections, and the reasons are not as complex or convoluted as most of the analyses that I read in the paper about the groups to which we must appeal or not appeal.

First, personality plays an enormous role in the choices that people make when they vote. Ronald Reagan is the epitome of that argument. Voters want to cast their ballots for people they trust, people they think care about them. That's really basic. All things being equal, you can take an inflammatory issue and you can cast serious doubts in people's minds about a candidate—and it was done very well in this last election—but if the organization is in place and the people have faith in the candidate, it will not destroy the campaign. Basically, people vote for people they like.

If you ask the American people what the Republican Party stands for and what Republicans believe, they will tell you that Republicans are for a strong defense, strong foreign policy, and a strong economy. If you ask them what the president does, what his responsibilities are, they will tell you that the president maintains a strong defense, conducts foreign policy, and gets a hold on the economy. The Republican Party has done a very good job of shaping their image around these "presidential" issues.

On the other hand, if you ask the American people what the Democratic Party stands for they will tell you the Democratic Party stands for good environmental protection, clean air and water, safety in the workplace, representation of the middle class and the poor, education, principally domestic issues. Ask them what Congress does and they will tell you Congress fights for our environment and clean air and water, protects the middle class and the poor, impacts on education, and generally takes care of domestic issues. So the people elect a Republican president and a Democratic Congress.

Now that's an overgeneralization, the one I heard first from my friend Alan Baron, but it is the analysis that makes the most sense to me.

It will be difficult for the Democratic Party to elect anyone outside the Washington beltway for president. The party needs a senator whose forte is defense, foreign policy, and the economy. Plus—and this is of prime importance—a winning personality. In this age of electronic eye contact there is a lot to be said for charisma.

It doesn't do a lot of good to sit around and muse about what's going to happen next. The suggestion that somehow the Democratic Party is dead because it doesn't run the presidency, when it continues to control most of the elections that are held in this country, is dead wrong. I wish we had won this last election, but we didn't, and it's time to move forward.

15

★

I
T was as if, socially, my life went into reverse. Before, it had been very important to me to bring people into my house, because that was my main exposure to the outside world. Now, whether through the job or speeches at night or the never-ending public appearances, I was constantly thrust into the outside world. My house, then, became the place where I could seek refuge. It was the opposite of the life I had led for so many years.

I was so bruised from the dissolution of my marriage that I think I'm still fearful of getting myself into a relationship where that could happen to me again. And so my social life assumed the quietest proportions.

For a while I played bridge with my friends Paula and Ernest Smith and Robert Spellings. Robert is a dear friend, but he met and married a darling woman who is not a bridge player, and when they married the bridge game went by the boards.

My truthful opinion about dating is that I'm not all that much fun to take out. Life in public has become a constant greeting of people wherever I go. If I go to a banquet or a dance I work most of the evening, meeting, greeting, shaking hands.

And by the time the evening is past nine o'clock I'd just as soon go home.

My kids have been really great. I love to go to the movies, I've always loved movies, so I see a lot of them with my son Dan and my daughter Ellen. Movies are dark and quiet, and no one talks to you. One of my favorite treats is to go to a Houston Rockets game with Gary Bradley.

I have some men friends that I go out with from time to time, but that's all it is, friendship. And that's okay. Life is rich for me.

We still have the annual Christmas Eve party at the house with all the kids and my closest friends. And I entertain now and then, but it's rare. I still like to cook but I don't have the time to do it. I cook for myself when I'm home, which isn't often. My personal life is so inextricably bound to my public life that my biggest problems are finding time to get my clothes to the cleaners and getting back to pick them up.

Frances Goff invites me to speak to the new group at Girls State each year. Frances is getting older but is still just as sharp as a tack and aggressive and tough and wonderful. She has probably inspired more girls to seek their full potential than any person I know.

When I speak to these girls I try not to talk about the glories of public office, because I figure that's what all the other speakers talk about. I talk to them about what it means to be female, and how they should think of themselves; what society is *really* going to give them, not what they *hope* society is going to give them. It's one of my favorite events each year.

I quote a line from the *Cinderella Complex* that *if* Prince Charming shows up, he isn't going to be on a white horse, he's going to be on a Honda and expect them to make the payments. Reality. I tell them that homemaking, if that's what you call what I did—"house engineering"—was, along with teaching school, the hardest work I ever performed. I tell them that they are encouraged to think that someone is going to take care of them, but that no one is.

I tell them that the one thing we are *not* encouraged to learn is how to take care of ourselves, how to take responsibility for our own lives. Taking responsibility for yourself is an enormous task. The love of friends and family is sustenance, the love of God gives spiritual guidance; they are invaluable sources of support, but they will not rescue you from yourself. The security derived from self-acceptance, self-reliance, provides the foundation for loving life.

I tell them that they will work harder and earn less doing the same thing that most men do—which is true. That many of their marriages will end in divorce—which is statistically true. That they can have a good and wonderful life, but that it only begins when they accept responsibility for it, not when they expect someone else to make it happen. They have never, ever, been confronted with such a message.

I tell them what it means to be a woman. In the present society it means that they have more doors open to them than at any time in the past. It means that they will have every opportunity for a good education if they are willing to expend the effort to get it. But it also means that unless they are extraordinarily good, or have some other real talent—or connections with money—they will reach a certain level in their professional life and it will be truly difficult for them to move higher. If they choose a profession of homemaking, it is important for them to become involved in their community and give balance to their lives so that they do not suffer from isolation.

I urge them to be full citizens, to be aware of the governmental issues that affect their lives. We are often told that politics is "dirty," that government is an institution that has little effect on us. The simple fact of the matter is that politics and government involve all of us—as homemakers, as women with professions, as retirees, as students, as children—whether we choose it or not.

Government touches every part of our lives: the quality of education we receive, the prices we pay at the grocery store, access to medical care, everything from garbage pickup to the most profound questions of life and death on the planet. There is no aspect of our lives so secure that it is shielded from the influence of public policy. I am impatient with the term "women's issues," which are assumed to revolve around whether we have babies or not. Women's issues are no different from the issues that affect all human beings.

On my forty-ninth birthday Claire Korioth put together a fund-raiser/costume party. Everyone was dressed in my old costumes, Wonder Woman, Santa Claus, the Wicked Witch of the West. And they all had masks with my face on them. It was pretty cute.

By the end of my first Treasury campaign we had run out of every piece of printed material we had; the signs, the brochures, the bumper stickers—everything was gone. We were in the little town of La Joya, in South Texas, where my good friend Billy Leo, and his father before him, Leo J. Leo, ran the general store. These tiny Texas towns are built right on the highway, and Billy Leo's store was next to a dirt patch that served as a parking lot. Next to that was the one-story building that served as the city hall and the senior citizens' center.

In all of these small South Texas towns there is a center called the Amigos del Valle, the "Friends of the Valley." These centers are where the elderly gather for a hot meal. But the Amigos del Valle are more than just places to get something to eat, they are the connection that the old people have with the community.

The man who runs the Amigos of the Valley is Amancio Chapa, and he really does run a fantastic program. Each year they crown a king and queen, and it is a big event. Each center sends a man and woman as its representatives, and the competition is stiff. I came for the crowning one time and it was fabulous; they were all so dressed up and having such a good time. The entertainment was Tito Guizar, who was a Mexican movie star years ago. He is in his late seventies and still tall and imposing, and the people were all very excited and thrilled that he was there.

Going into centers like the Amigos, where they are doing handicrafts and playing dominoes, you want to stop and say, "What I ought to be doing the rest of my life is working here." They are so appreciative that you have come, and it makes you realize how little most people ask of life.

These people have worked hard all their lives, raised families, and now they are really poor and getting old. They don't want a lot of money, they don't want to go a lot of places, they don't want a lot of things; they just want human warmth and affection.

We had gone to the Amigos del Valle center in La Joya and I had talked with the people there. I think Hobby was on that trip, and maybe Hightower. The old folks were so pleased if you gave them something that had your picture on it, and I was out of material; we had given away everything we had. Cecile was with me, and she remembered the masks. They were in the back of the van, so she went and got them and we gave them away.

It was late afternoon by the time we were going to leave, kind of dusky on the highway. And as we were pulling away I saw a little woman, she couldn't have been over four and a half feet tall, probably in her early eighties, standing by the highway waiting for her ride. She was a frail woman in a cotton print dress that hung straight to her ankles.

I really thought, looking out that window, that that little woman is what our business of public service is all about. She has faith in us to do right by her and by the place where she lives. She will never know the intricacies, the machinations, the pull and tug and harshness of politics, and it doesn't matter. What she does need to know is that there are people serving in public office who care about her and her community. That's all she needs to know.

And it's important that we be true to her. Because, in the big fights and big issues over how money is spent, if we lose sight of these people we have really lost sight of our goal.

She had a mask. She was standing in front of Billy Leo's store wearing my face. I waved at her. She waved back.

PHOTO CREDITS

★

1. Ann Richards' personal collection
2. Ann Richards' personal collection
3. Ann Richards' personal collection
4. John Huber
5. Ann Richards' personal collection
6. Ann Richards' personal collection
7. T. W. Powers
8. Ann Richards' personal collection
9. Ann Richards' personal collection
10. Carrin Patman
11. DiMicco/Ferris Studio
12. Bill Leissner
13. Frank Micelotta/Time
14. Alan Pogue